TO BEARS AND WOLVES

TREE HOUSE

VICTORY GARDEN

JOHN AND MELANIE
BOBBY AND BENNY

CHARLIE AND
AUGUSTA MYERS
ON THE NEXT
RIDGE

JEN
MAGIC
TEA HOUSE
IN ALDER
PATCH

WILD FLOWER
MEADOW

CARL AND
JILLIAN'S

BUTCH   JASON

1" RIGHT OF
WAY

NEIL GOODMAN'S
UPPER FIELD

GOODMAN'S OLD
FARMYARD

MOOSE
FLAT

CLIFF'S PLACE
IN THE FLAT

MOOSE
CREEK

CREEK

THE
PLACE
CREEK

100 MILES
TO HOMER

THE
BRIDGE

FRAM'S
CORNER

BILL
O'LEARY'S

JARED'S

TO CURD'S
SLAUGHTER
HOUSE

POST OFFICE
SLEEPING
MOOSE

BRIAN
AND ANNA
TANNER'S

100 MILES
TO ANCHORAGE

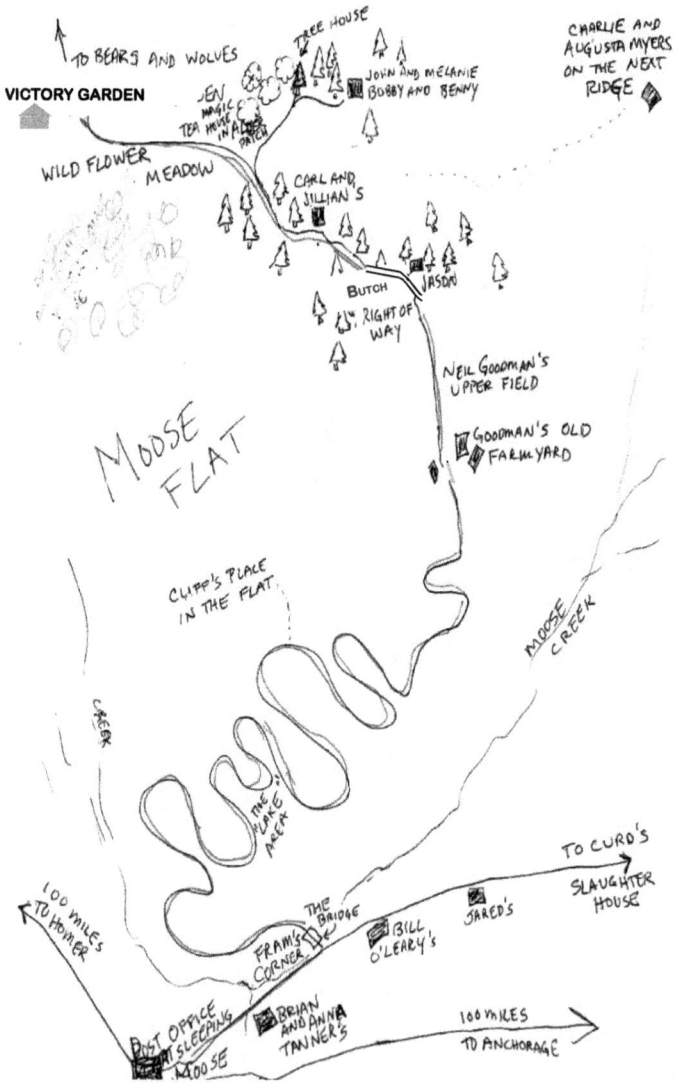

SLEEPING MOOSE

Round Top Road from end to end (not to scale).

ELEPHANT

in the BUSH

with Conclusions—

Sleeping Moose Saga

—Part Three

by ATWOOD CUTTING

Elephant in the Bush
With Conclusions
Sleeping Moose Saga Part Three

—by Atwood Cutting

3rd Edition
ISBN: 978-09975819-1-1

Publisher's Cataloging-In-Publication Data
(Prepared by The Donohue Group, Inc.)

Names: Cutting, Atwood. | Cutting, Atwood. Tales
    from Sleeping Moose. Volumes 3-4.
Title: Elephant in the bush / with conclusions by
    Atwood Cutting.
Description: Colorado Springs, CO: Cutting/Echo
    Hill Arts Press, LLC, [2016] | Series:
    Sleeping Moose saga; part 2 | "Substantial
    revision of Tales from Sleeping Moose, Volumes
    3-4, which were originally released in 2015."
Identifiers: LCCN 2016943610 | ISBN 978-0-
    9975819-1-1 (softcover)
Subjects: LCSH: Frontier and pioneer life--
    Alaska--History--20th century--Fiction. |
    Adventure and adventurers--Alaska--History--
    20th century--Fiction. | Families--Alaska--
    History--20th century--Fiction. | Alaska--
    Social life and customs--20th century--
    Fiction. | LCGFT: Historical fiction.
Classification: LCC PS3603.U88 E44 2016 | DDC
    813/.6--dc23

These events all happened, but
the locations and characters have been fictionalized.
Any resemblance to actual persons or places
is coincidental.

This saga is dedicated to
all kind-hearted souls who long for
a sweeter, simpler world, and to seekers of
Camelot, world peace, or any other good
but impossible dream.

Big thanks to
my collaborating editor and friend, Dee Fischer.
My appreciation also to Rebecca Hinebough, George Read,
Mr. Caye, and to Suze, who worked at Bell's Nursery,
wherever you are. To the sculptor who crafted the rearing
elephant in homage to all pioneers (visitors can see the
elephant at The California Trail Interpretive Center in Elko,
Nevada) and to the anonymous photographer who captured
those two darling oxen in love, *mahalo*.

Atwood Cutting

"The clearest way into the universe is through a forest wilderness."
—John Muir, **Naturalist**

"I lived alone, in the woods, a mile from any neighbor, in a house which I had built myself."
—Henry David Thoreau

— Contents —

—1—

Two Winters in Fairbanks

"Dorm" Life in Pictures

AFTER THE HARROWING winters and springs of '79 and '80, the Peters family headed north to spend the next two winters serving as Resident Advisors of an eight-story student-housing facility on the University of Alaska campus.

While they were there, Kate wrote to Mamasan less often and kept fewer journal notes, partly because she was plenty busy with the two-hundred twenty-seven residents who called her "Mom," and partly because she now had all the comforts of home, and felt no need to record her struggles to survive while at the college. Kate also had a telephone at her disposal and, since it was so much more fun to talk with the wiser, older woman back home than to send letters, she did so almost weekly. Thus, written records are scarce. But the following photographs should tell the story well.

"Two roads diverged in a wood—and I—I took the one less traveled by, and that has made all the difference."
—Robert Frost, 20th Century Poet

Isolated in central Alaska, Fairbanks is the gateway to many an odyssey.

Rural Alaska Natives, whose ancestors have lived in the Arctic for millennia, might be accustomed to the remoteness and the cold. But Fairbanks, the largest population conglomeration around, will present temptations and situations never before encountered. Meanwhile, most "cheechakos" newly up from the Lower Forty-Eight envision Fairbanks as a place to drop over the edge of civilization in search of adventure—or solitude—or perhaps to settle into a world of freedom from social norms and the bounds of Hammurabi's paradigms for civil order. Either way, Fairbanks—at the end of the road—is exotic.

Fairbanks, on the Chena River,
is an isolated outpost in Alaska's interior.

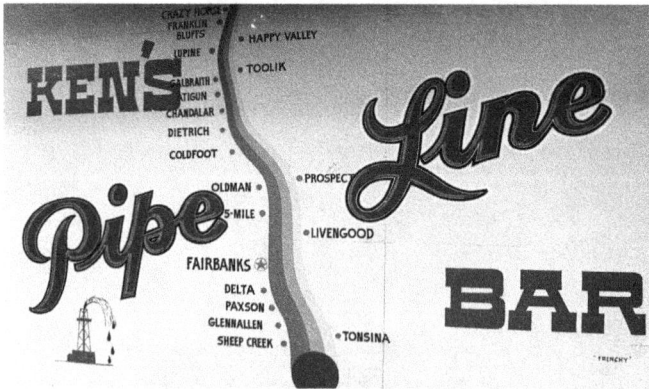

In the 1970s, the Trans-Alaska Pipeline
roared in and recharged the nearly forgotten gold town.

The following photographs were taken at the
University of Alaska, Fairbanks, in the early 1980s.

An unfinished bridge leading to woods begged to be explored.

A variety of vehicles cruised the campus.

*For students from the **Native** villages, the typical*
university life must have felt foreign, while many of the
more rambunctious youths from "outside" played
for as long as the summer days shed their generous sunlight.

Meanwhile, a few spirited characters experimented with creative ways of avoiding cabin fever.

*Then came the snow games which waned with the dying sunlight as the deep **Arctic** winter settled in.*

Only adventurous souls remained to
experience this legendary season of cold.

While students braved the steepest hills on campus, little Atwood enjoyed the lower, slower slopes.

Finally, fall semester ended. The Peters family was more than ready to head south for a Christmas mountain break.

After Christmas, they traveled north again—like a pendulum.

On cold and windless days, Fairbanks was shrouded in ice fog (instantly frozen carbon monoxide) and campus power plant plumes rose straight up as though starched.

*But Kate had come north from Hawaii to see
just such a winter as this. With hoarfrost-laden branches playing
in front of the sunrise-sunset show, each day offered a pleasant
three-hour display all tinted in apricot and peach—
and glittering, to boot.*

* * *

One day, Kate absentmindedly shut the driver's side door a little too hard and the door handle snapped off. It was somewhere around sixty below zero, too cold for anything but whispered breaths around cold metal, she remembered belatedly. Although they now had to use the passenger door for entrance and egress, Tim kept the engine running and the tires pressurized, and he never once reprimanded her.

They were nearing the end of their second winter as residence hall advisors at the university, and they had a second child due that spring. All was going smoothly. Why sweat the small stuff?

Tim loved their chartreuse Gremlin, despite its unfortunate proportions and flattened fenders. It faithfully hauled the family between Fairbanks and Sleeping Moose for a penny-a-mile.

3/10/82, Fairbanks—Dear Mamasan,

Light snow is wafting down this afternoon. Temps are nearly always above zero now. Spring can't be far away. ("Oh boy, there must be a horse around here somewhere!" the little optimist cried out with glee!)

Tim is home for his two-week break. He and Attie are out getting new tires (and probably ice cream cones). I think it's working out well, this typical Alaskan lifestyle. He'll be gone half the time, but when he's home he'll be resting, and he'll have plenty of time to be a marvelous daddy and husband.

We're looking forward to leaving the dorm job, though. It'll be wonderful spending time together up on the mountain again. We probably won't be getting rich any day soon, but Tim likes the work and says it's a "gold mine" of connections. Soon we could live anywhere there's an oil industry. (Maybe Curaçao or Djakarta???)

Little unborn babe kicks restlessly at the gate. Unless he/she comes early, we're scheduled for an April 6 arrival. Tim gets home on the 5th, and I'll have already checked myself into the hospital. He gets off the plane, takes a taxi to the hospital, visits me, and drives the car home. Pretty slick, huh? (Peggy at the dorm will be babysitting Attie.)

      Then, the next day—poof!
      We're really excited.

      If baby should tire of waiting and jump the gun, there are many people around here who have offered their assistance. Don't worry about me needing you before the big event, but having you come to Fairbanks to help out when Tim goes back up to Prudhoe Bay will really be great. Attie will be needing a special friend right about then.

      Much aloha, T, K, A, and ?

P.S. I can well imagine that you were tired of being pregnant by the time your last one came along. It's a slow, uncomfortable process growing a baby. Not to mention rearing the child after that. Yet, we continue to do it.

Neil Brewster Joins the Family

WHEN NEIL BREWSTER was born, they proudly carried him home in their little green chariot. There, they discovered a huge banner that some of the dorm's leading miscreants had suspended above the door of the building. It said:

"It's a boy! Archibald Angus."

Oh, those college smarties . . .

It's a boy! Archibald Angus

Grandma Tutu came up to play with Attie.

Attie and Baby Brew became acquainted.

Frampton in the News

"HEY TIM! LISTEN to this: Frampton is in the news!" Kate read aloud from the Fairbanks Daily News Miner. "Squatter Frampton Snyder has been ordered by Alaska Superior Court Judge Cromwell Smythe to leave his ten-acre homesite near Sleeping Moose in the central Kenai Peninsula."

She handed off the paper to Tim so he could read the whole article for himself.

It turned out that the spot by the bridge where Frampton set up wasn't part of the 160-acres Goodman had been granted back in 1958. Thanks in great part to Jillian's letter-writing campaign, the illegality had come to light, and Fram had now been duly ordered to leave. The minor census adjustment from the Snyder family's departure, alone would mean some big changes around there.

"It should make things a lot easier," Kate said, thrilled at the news. "A lot less junk lying around at the bridge."

"A lot less manure to drive through," Tim added.

At that moment the Peterses were still in Fairbanks, but they would be heading back to Sleeping Moose—with a new baby—in just a couple of months. The thought of driving up a nice, clear road again made both of them smile.

May 15, 1982—Dear Mamasan,

Another winter is nearly over.

We'll be headed to the mountain soon.

Our neighbor Fram lost his court battle, so he'll be leaving That's a huge headache gone. I can't wait to see the creek area all clean again. Once he and his animals are gone, that blight will be nothing but a memory.

It doesn't feel very virtuous to be so relieved by his plight, but we really need to protect our home, right?

Love, KTA and little Brew

Homecoming

Saying goodbye to ballet classes and friends in Fairbanks.

BY LATE JUNE, the Peters family was headed home. Approaching the bridge, Tim and Kate were hoping that the Snyders had moved on.

After two tiring days in the car the pilgrims arrived at the creek. The Snyders hadn't gone anywhere! Darn. *There* sat Frampton, on his stump, as usual. He looked perfectly comfortable to be sitting there, too. What a colossal disappointment!

"Look who's hanging around like a fart in the phone booth," Tim muttered.

"Shouldn't he be cleared out of here by now?" Kate whispered back.

They were both a little worried to see Fram sitting there, since he'd been legally evicted quite recently and he might be irritated after all the hullabaloo.

"How's the family?" Tim asked, opting to stay on Fram's good side.

"Fine, jest fine. We got a new little one, name o' Orvis. Looks like his dad."

Poor kid, Kate thought privately.

"Say, who's that in there?" Frampton was peering into the car at the Peterses' newest addition. All he could see was a little head, as sweet as a peach, poking out over the top of a baby pouch tied to Kate's chest. "This is Brewster, Atwood's little brother. He was born up in Fairbanks."

"You don't say." Fram scrutinized the sack of baby for a moment. The hair was so blond that the kid looked totally bald. "That boy's got no hair," he observed.

Then he turned and spoke to Tim. "Say, speakin' o' boys, my bull has wandered off. Let me know if you see him up your way, will ya?"

"Sure will," Tim promised. Then, having stopped just long enough to be civil, he put the car in gear and headed away with a noncommittal, "See you later."

Kate shook her head as soon as they were around the bend. "This makes me nervous."

"Don't worry, babe. You can shoot a gun. If he comes up to our door and looks like he wants to walk in over your dead body, you just shoot first."

"Oh, well *now* I'm relieved." She shivered as she thought of the day Frampton Snyder had first driven into their world. She still regretted having said such fighting words, but there was just something about him that elicited a visceral response from a lot o' folks, including Kate.

"Anyway," Tim said, "he won't be up here much longer. The courts have spoken. Now it's only a matter of time."

"How long do you think it'll take to get Fram out of here, lock, stock and barrel?"

"That might be easier said than done. There aren't many State Troopers around here to enforce the law. Remember how it took three days for a trooper to show up at the Curd place? And *that was a shooting.* It's possible Fram could end up staying where he is until *he* decides he's ready to go. Which might be forever. Face it: folks in town hope he stays up on this mountain, out of sight and out of mind," Tim said. And he was probably right.

"Heck, if a person could still homestead, *we'd* have homesteaded," Kate groused. "But we *paid* for our farm, while Fram just *moved in*. He's a squatter, plain and simple. It's not fair. But mostly why I want him *gone* is because he keeps such a messy camp. I'll always be a Girl Scout at heart."

"We'll just have to wait and see what happens next," Tim said.

They bumped up their road, longing for the day when they could put Frampton Snyder out of their minds the way folks in town had done.

When they got to the Goodmans' abandoned farmyard, they saw that a fire had damaged the place over that winter. The big barn was half burnt, and the little loaf-shaped house had partially caved in.

It was sad to see all those wonderful memories now scarred and broken—all those great meals and legendary tales. They drove between the crushed Twinkie and the old outhouse and then started across the upper field. "I guess that was caused by lightning."

"Probably," Tim responded. He punched the Gremlin through the last section of roller-coaster mud holes and woods, skirted Carl and Jillian's turnoff, then wove up through the wildflowers that led to their front door. They were home.

Kate eased out first, and then Tim and Attie followed, using the passenger door which was now the only one that opened. After stretching, they walked over to stand in front of the split flights of main stairs. One went up to the great room and the other led down to the basement.

Attie held onto her mommy's pant leg, and Kate held Brew's tiny head to keep it from lolling from side to side over the top of the pouch as Tim unlocked the padlock on the basement door. He pulled the latch string, and went inside. His family waited as he went up the interior stairs and came around to unlock the strong east door and usher them into the great room.

Kate and Attie stepped inside. The big room smelled chilly but not moldy. It looked intact. Everything looked exactly the way they'd left it.

They'd been gone all fall, winter, and spring for the past two years, and still the house stood sound and ready to welcome them home. Excellent!

Kate laid Brew on the couch and started rolling up the window quilts, one by one. Attie, glad to be out of the car and finally able to move, jumped into each magic square of sunlight that appeared as Kate removed the window coverings. It had been a long winter, and the long-darkened room seemed happy to open itself up to the sudden sunshine.

"Hey, Kate. Come an' look at this!" Tim shouted from somewhere down the hall. "I guess we *did* have visitors, after all."

Kate followed his voice around the corner and found him down the hall staring at the back door. The top half of the door— where six glass panes used to be—had a big piece of cardboard nailed over it. There was a note tucked under one edge of the cardboard.

> HELLO.   FEB. 14, 1982
> WE WERE SKIING AND GOT CAUGHT IN A BLIZZARD.
> SORRY WE HAD TO BREAK YOUR WINDOWS TO GET IN.
> HOPE THIS PAYS FOR THE GLASS.
> YOUR HOUSE SAVED OUR LIVES. THANK YOU!

The couple had signed their names, and when Tim took down the note, a twenty-dollar-bill fluttered to the floor.

"Hmm," Tim said.

"Well, well," Kate echoed his surprise.

"They're lucky this place was here," Tim said.

"You're not kidding," Kate agreed. "It's too bad the window panes will be a hassle for you; but it does feel good to know that our house saved two lives." She tried to picture the stranded visitors' reaction. Had they been astounded at the fine workmanship they had stumbled upon (or into)? "I wonder what they thought when they saw it inside."

Tim, who was busy considering the task of reglazing the windows, answered absent-mindedly.

"They were probably relieved."

"I mean, when they saw the beams and the tile mosaic under the stove, did they notice how extra-beautiful this place is?"

"I don't know for sure. But I *am* sure they were relieved." Tim considered her question "They probably wondered how we got our ridgepole up there."

The memory of that particular feat made Kate snort. "Yeah, *I* still wonder how we got it up there, too."

When Tim went back to the great room and opened the door of the wood stove, he found three broken fire bricks inside. "They must have burned coal in this thing," he said. "It got so hot that some of the bricks cracked."

"That's too bad," Kate lamented. "Let's hope it still works."

Tim laid a fire in the little Jøtul stove and lit it. Then he watched carefully until he was sure it was safe to burn, and pronounced it so. "It looks like we'll be okay,"

Kate reviewed the events of their trip. "The best thing about this whole day is that we're home again, and everything is right where we left it. And *nearly* intact."

A whimper came from Brew.

"Oh, you're hungry, aren't you?" she said to her baby boy. Responding to their primal purpose, her breasts prickled. Kate lifted her infant out of his pouch carrier and went over to take a seat in the old recliner.

Brew's baby blues filled with gratitude and his lips began to suck in anticipation. That ageless cue caused her milk to let down, and as two wet blobs appeared on her shirt front, she settled in to nurse him.

Baby Boy Brewster nudged into her breast and began guzzling with fervor. He worked hard, until he could hold no more and his grip loosened. Then his little head dropped away, and he was asleep. After gently burping him, Kate laid her babe in his crib. She swaddled him warmly. It would be a long time before the heat of the now-warming stove reached this room.

Turning at the hall door, she watched his plump lips give one last suck of satisfaction, and left him to nap.

Pretty soon Kate made supper, and the three sat on beam-butt stools to dine close to the fire.

It would take a day or two to get the chill out of the place, but *Lordy,* it was good to be home!

This is the house that Tim built.

−2−

All the Comforts

Phone and Water

"THAT'S US," TIM said, as soon as he'd started reading the letter. "This is from the phone company."

Their name had been on the telephone company's list for the past six years.

In June the government issued a federal grant to provide telephone service to every rural customer on the list and the Peterses' number had finally come up!

June 27, 1982—Dear Mama,

A note to you while this gorgeous baby is nursing. (Please excuse the scrawl.) Thank you for teaching me the one-handed child-hold. It's always useful when I need to pour water.

We're home on the farm safe and sound. Tim is so happy to be back. He loves it here.

Someone broke into our house while we were away. They had to, to stay alive. It was a couple of skiers who got surprised by a blizzard. They're lucky they found our place. The weather around here can kill a guy (as we now know).

News flash, I think we're about to get a phone! I'll call you when (if) we do.

On July 7, right after Tim left for the ARCO oilfield at Prudhoe Bay (he was now working an alternating two-weeks-on / two-weeks-off schedule), the phone crew arrived, all ready to hook them up. When they were finished, one of the fellows handed Kate a phone book and told her they were at the end of the rural party line, which reminded her of the day they'd gotten electricity more than five years before. They were at the end of their electrical line, too.

The crew boss assigned them a special arrangement of rings and then the men headed back down the mountain.

Those old hobbles of isolation started popping off Kate's ankles before the installation crew had even made it into the forest. First, she dialed the Medivac helicopter service and asked them to put the name "Peters," and their location, on the map. Just knowing there was a little red pushpin pointing to them right there on the rescue crew's wall was an instant source of comfort to the mother of two.

Next, she called Hawaii. "Hi, Mamasan. Guess where I'm calling from . . ."

Kate told her mother about the helicopter evacuation plan she had just implemented, and Grandma Tutu said she was very happy with this latest development. Then Attie got to say "Hi" and "Bye," and Kate hung up before she ran up a huge long-distance phone bill.

Her third call was to a well driller in Footprint.

Kate just up and did it. She wanted running water, and she could tell Tim about it later. She figured they could use their first oil dividend checks (courtesy of Alaska's recent oil revenues) to pay for it. Brewster's birth in April had bumped their family's census up to four. At $1,000 apiece, that gave them a cool $4,000 to work with. It would be like getting a well drilled for free. So, she made the call.

When Tim came home a few days later and she told him about it, he was genuinely pleased to hear of her exploit.

* * *

That Monday morning their phone rang its first ring. Kate answered.

"Hello? Yes, this is the lady of the house" (a wink to Tim). "No, we don't." (She listened to a long spiel.) "Well, we live pretty far out" (a short pause). "I'm not sure you know what you're promising. It would be difficult to deliver your paper to our door. I think you'd need a helicopter."

The caller said something after that, and Kate let him go gently. "I understand completely. But thanks for calling." And she hung up.

Tim was curious. "Who was that?"

"Somebody who wanted to deliver the Anchorage Daily News to our front door."

"Did you sign us up?"

She looked sideways at him and gave a sarcastic little, "Ha-ha."

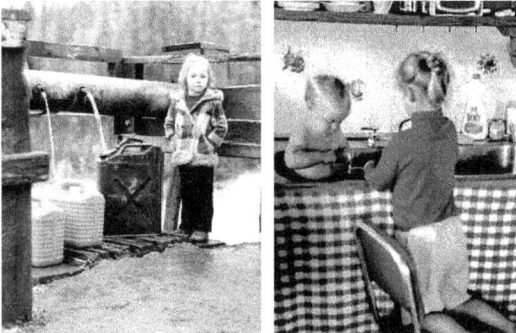

Big sister Attie liked to help her mama get water at the spring. She also kept Brew entertained in his bath.

* * *

The well-driller came up just after Tim had gone back to work.

"Have you had the place witched yet?" the man with the drill asked.

"No. Do I need to do that?" "Well I'm not touching it 'til it's been witched," he said.

"Okay. Where do I get a "Witcher"? Kate was standing out in the field, with a baby on each hip.

"A guy I know can do it for you. I can tell 'im to come up here if you want."

"Yes, I want. Please ask him to come."

"Okay, but I won't touch it 'til he's witched it," the old-timer repeated sourly. "And maybe you could ask your neighbor down at the bridge to clear the road. My truck barely made it past that freezer he has parked on the bend." He looked at Kate and her two children and bobbed his head in parting.

Kate nodded good-day as he hoisted himself back into the oversized truck with a drill-arm mount and lumbered it away.

A couple of days later the well-driller returned with a fellow named Joe in tow. Tim still wasn't home, so Kate took the children along with her and walked outside to oversee the process.

"Where do you want me to look?" Joe asked. He had two rods in hand.

Kate pointed down between her feet. "How about right here?"

Joe shrugged and said, "Okay." The dowser held his arms out in front of his chest and let the brass rods drift freely across each other, demonstrating their own divine inclinations. Kate thought those rods looked willing to go pretty much whichever way Joe wanted them to go, but *maybe* there was something to it. Magnetic attraction, maybe? Who was she to say?

The three adults stood watching the brass rods swing across each other, until baby Brew began whimpering for some lunch. Kate began to worry that her milk would let down before a drilling location had been decided upon. Attie was pulling on Kate's pant leg, Brew was whimpering, and mosquitoes were buzzing.

When the wands had done all the work they were inclined to do, the diviner let his arms fall to his sides. The show was over. Joe sauntered to his truck, folded up the rods, and slipped them into a leather case lying on the driver's seat. From there on, it would be up to the driller.

The two men conferred briefly, and then Joe scrawled something on a piece of paper and handed it to Kate.

> Pay to Joe Bush
> $75 for dowsing.
> 8/4/82

Kate, with Attie welded to her like a third leg, waddled awkwardly over to the truck hood, so she could use it as a desk, and began writing out a check. After she'd handed it to the rod-man, he got into his truck to wait for his friend so they could get on home.

But the driller was still standing there, giving Kate a disgusted stare. He seemed to come to a decision before he folded his arms across his chest disapprovingly.

"You young gals, you say you're wantin' to rough it when you move way out here. And then, the first thing you know, you're wantin' electricity, and then water, and I don't know what all else." He paused and looked exasperated. "Can you tell me just what in the hell you're doin' out here, anyway?"

Kate was struck dumb for a moment. Then the pioneer's wife wearing two children looked straight back at the man and said coolly, "Sir, I am just coping."

By now Attie was yanking at her mother's pant leg, begging to be picked up. Brew was crying openly, as hungry as a bear in spring, and Kate's milk was leaking down through her shirtfront like an impaled cactus.

The driller grunted, but he didn't say another word on the subject. "Well, you've got water here, all right," he finally allowed.

"Good," Kate said, not a bit surprised. With their spring so close by, she'd figured they were probably sitting on top of an underground lake.

"When can you start drilling?"
"I can be back next week."
"Okay, good. Thanks."

The well-man got into "Witcher" Joe's truck and the two bounced off down the road. Kate watched them disappear behind the buffer of wilderness that separated her world from all the crowds that lived out there on the other side. Then she hauled her screaming children into the house and gave them lunch.

* * *

A week later the driller guy came back, as promised, and he drilled for three straight days.

When his drill hit water at one hundred feet on the nose, the old fellow retracted his boom-arm bit, filled out a slip on a pad, and tore out a page. He drove his truck over to the house and honked at the front door.

Kate came out, and he handed her a bill for $2,300 and pulled away into the mist.

Kate watched the man's truck disappear into a drizzling rain. Then she grabbed her slicker and went outside to take a good look at the new well.

There wasn't much to see: a pipe sticking up out of the ground. That was all there was. What was she supposed to do with that? Use a tin cup on a string? Kate decided that *she* could take care of the babies, and *Tim* could take care of the water from this point on.

* * *

As soon as Tim got home from the oilfield on the North Slope, Kate showed him the capped well, all the while fretting about having spent over two thousand dollars on such an unimpressive result. But Tim looked happy.

"You just leave it to me," he said. "I'll have this thing up and running in no time."

So, Kate left it to Tim as she went inside to fix supper and continue coping.

* * *

Tim spent the entire two weeks of his R&R toiling to get that water going. First, he sank a pump down to the bottom of the well. Then he dug a trench six feet deep all the way from the house to the well. He connected a pipe to the stub left behind by the well-driller, and then he backfilled the trench. He spent the next three days puttering around down in the basement. Finally, he moved his operation upstairs and edged his way in under the sink.

* * *

"Kate, can you come over here and help me for a second?" Tim was awkwardly scrunched under the newly framed-in double sinks.

Kate put down the baby and went to see what her husband wanted. "What do you need?"

She was surprised to be looking at two new faucets rising up out of a newly-built counter with twin stainless-steel sinks. "Hey, hey, hey," the delighted lady cheered. "Now, this is promising!"

It looked like her running water was getting closer.

"I need you to turn on the cold-water faucet," he said.

Kate hesitated, not expecting a miracle but *hoping* for one, anyway.

"Go ahead," Tim prodded. "Turn it on."

Kate gave the faucet a turn. At her command, a series of burps and gurgles began echoing through the pipes.

"Turn it off," Tim said.

She quickly turned off the faucet.

Tim worked for a few more minutes under the sink, and then he asked her to turn on the faucet again.

She did so.

A gush of muddy water belched out of the virgin spout.

"Oh my gosh!" Kate was awestruck.

Pretty soon the belches started to smooth out and a stream of water as clear as Saran Wrap flowed from the new spigot. "Okay, turn it off," he said.

"Oh Tim, we have running water! Oh, thank you, thank you. *Thank you!*" She was gushing. "I am so happy!" Right then she was thinking: This is a *good man* I married, *one heck of a good man!*

It was wonderful having water at her fingertips, even though she had to use the tap sparingly. Since they were still carting all dirty water out in the slop bucket, "rationing" was the word to remember. If that can overflowed, the kitchen would flood.

While Tim was next away at work, Kate painted the counters and tiled the whole countertop.

* * *

The following R&R, Tim and Kate dug a big hole for the cesspool. Tim ran a drainpipe from the house out to the hole, and they covered it with logs and sod. When he told Kate that she would never again have to carry water in—*or out*—she knew her life had taken a definite turn for the better. For three whole days she didn't ask for anything more.

Then, one morning after an almost not-fast-enough run to the outhouse, her hankering for an indoor toilet flushed anew. It's not like she was asking for much: they already had an old used stool. She'd bought it at a garage sale and carted it home, fully expecting to have it installed before winter. That had been five years ago, and the promising fixture still hadn't been resuscitated. She decided she'd ask Tim about it when he came home from the Slope.

* * *

"Why don't we bring that old flush up here and plumb it in while you're home?" she suggested on his first morning back. She knew Tim could do this. Tim could do *anything*!

"Not so fast. We're not ready for a toilet yet," he said.

"*I'm* ready for a toilet," the woman quickly corrected him.

"Oh, you are, huh?"

"Yes, I am."

He smiled at her. "Well, I guess we could take a look at it and see what it needs."

That was close enough to a "yes" for Kate. She headed for the door and beat a path down to the old fixture. It was still parked under the alder right beside the outhouse, as it had been since 1977.

Tim followed Kate down the hill with a little bit less enthusiasm, but when he got to the porcelain bowl, he knelt down and gave it a cursory inspection.

"Let's carry it up to the house so I can work on it in the basement," he said.

Kate got ready to lift.

"Now remember, once we lift it, no matter what happens, don't let go."

"Aye-aye, Chief."

Kate grabbed one side and Tim took the other, and together they hoisted their trophy six inches off the ground and started the awkward carry uphill to the house.

All the alder dust or pollen or whatever had made the thing unexpectedly slick and Kate's hold was slippery. Ten steps into the transfer the tarnished tank tumbled and plummeted to the ground.

"You let go!" Tim barked.

"It slipped." Kate said, feeling foolish.

"I told you to hold on tight."

"Yes, you did. And I dropped my end. Believe me, I am extremely sorry."

Tim cooled down immediately. "That's okay. We weren't really ready for a toilet."

"*I* was ready for a toilet," Kate said again.

"Be patient, my love. Someday I'll buy you a brand-new commode."

"Oh, be still my heart!" Kate said, feigning a swoon into her hero's arms.

* * *

In late September, Tim changed jobs at ARCO. Now he would be working on the North Slope ten weeks straight, with two weeks off at Christmas. This new assignment meant much bigger bucks, which they needed badly, but it also meant that Kate and the children would be left alone on the mountain all through the fall.

Now that they had water and a phone, things should be easy enough to manage. But Tim was hoping to make one final home improvement before he left Kate to cope alone for the next ten weeks. One morning the whole Peters family went down to the Outfitter & Supply in Footprint, where they milled around in the camping section.

"Hey, look here. Would this work?" He was pointing to a carton with a life-sized photo of a portable camp toilet on the side. Kate and the babies came over to consider the possibility.

"Hmmm. It just might do. It says it holds up to three gallons," Kate said as she calculated how many full coffee cans that would equal, and how many freezing trips to the outdoor can it would avoid. The numbers worked out pretty well. "Yeah. This might do nicely. And it's a simple low box, so Attie can learn to use it, too."

"Well, then I'm buying it, then. Nothing is too good for my queen."

"Hah! A throne for the queen!"

They purchased the luxury item and triumphantly carted it home.

* * *

"Well?" Tim asked. He'd been waiting while Kate went down the hall to the orange room and tried it out.

"It works fine," Kate said, smiling.

"Good. Now you've got all the comforts of a modern home."

"Yeah. That's just what the well-driller said."

"Oh, don't mind him. What does he know? You just keep on coping, babe," Tim said.

"Okay."

Then her mood became more serious. "Tim, what if we have a medical emergency up here while you're gone?"

"You shouldn't have any problems. You have the phone. And our place has its red pin on the map. If there's an emergency, you call for a helicopter."

"What if it's during a snowstorm, and they can't land?"

"You take the Skidoo into town."

"And if I can't get it to start?"

"Take the snowshoes."

. . . And there you had it.

"I'm not sure I could carry both children all the way down to the car, but I guess I could pull them in the sled."

"That's my girl," Tim said. "Always thinking."

Tim had done what he could to provide for his family, and now he would have to leave them to fend for themselves while he worked to keep them fed. Not all that different from prehistoric days . . .

* * *

When it was time to take their daddy to Soldotna and put him on a plane, Attie cried and Kate stood waving good-bye until the twin-engine Otter had circled town and was headed on its way to Fairbanks.

Then Kate hitched Brew's carrier up higher on her chest, and they turned for the car. "Well, kids, there goes Daddy. We're on our own now. What do you say we go home?"

"I miss Daddy," Attie whined and shuffled her feet.

"I know, baby. We all do. Let's go now. Maybe we can have pancakes for supper."

"Yum! I love pancakes!" Attie's spirits picked up instantly, as did her pace.

Once home, the three had pancakes and then passed a quiet evening in front of the woodstove, waiting for the telephone to ring. Tim had promised to call as soon as he got settled in a hotel in Fairbanks. Finally, Kate put the babies to bed and, at about ten that evening, Tim called.

"Yup. I'm here. I plan to show up for the union call tomorrow morning. I'll let you know where I'm headed as soon as I get dispatched."

"Okay, darlin'. We all love you and miss you."

"You just keep that portable-potty seat warm."

"You can bet on that! And you keep safe."

"You, too. I'll be back in ten weeks."

"You'll be back for Christmas, right?"

"Yup. I should be. Don't worry, now."

"Okay. You neither."

"Have you got those snowshoes handy?"

"They're right here, all greased up and ready to go."

"Okay then. I'll phone you after the union call and tell you where I'm bound."

"Okay, babe. Sleep tight."

"You too. Good night. Say goodnight to the kids for me."

"They're both asleep, but I'll give them a kiss for you."

"Okay. You give them a kiss. Good night. I love you."

"Good night, Timber. I love you, too." After they hung up, a brilliant aurora hovered overhead, and the strange crackling sound it made bridged the silent night between them.

Kate banked the fire and went to bed, trying not to think of the wild things that lurked outside. The bed was cold when she climbed into it: no Timber to warm her feet. She shivered until she and the chilled sheets had reached the same temperature. For the next ten weeks even *getting into bed* would be hard. Ten weeks was a long time to be without your partner.

"I can handle it," she told herself. She'd have to handle it. This was bush life. Augusta Myers had tried to warn her.

Five hundred miles to the north, Tim sank onto an unfamiliar bed and fluffed his pillow, trying not to think about his family and the dangers that circled around them. He was far away now, and they were on their own.

* * *

October 4—Dear Tutu,

Your darling granddaughter just brought me a glass of water. She's my little water-bearer. She likes being able to turn the faucet on and off, and so do I.

I wish I could be talking to you on the telephone, but we got our phone bill last month: WOW! So, it'll be letters, as usual, for the most part. Okay?

I'll mail this next shower day.

Love, K, A and B

With her new portable can all warm and waiting right down the hall, Kate used the appliance as often as she pleased, reveling at the ease. From now on, the outhouse could be relegated to "warm, fair weather visits" exclusively, and that suited her just fine.

* * *

About a week after Tim's departure, Kate went to empty the camp commode for the first time. That's when her new contraption's biggest drawback reared its ugly head.

As soon as she'd released the dump cap, a putrid stench escaped from the magic box and nearly knocked her over.

"Wow!" Kate gagged. "Whoo-eey! That's *bad!*" She grabbed a breath from over her shoulder and began the emptying process.

"Steady, girl," she told herself. She was holding the foul bucket away at arm's length over the privy hole, and watching a stream of black lumpy stew dribble and plop its way into the pit. Kate tried not to inhale for the duration of the dumping procedure, but it was taking so long that she guessed she might die either way—by holding her breath, or by *not* holding her breath.

When her arms and lungs threatened to give out, the light-headed pioneer gave the box one last shake and then screwed the lid back on as fast as she could and carted the repulsive repository back up to the house.

"Well, that was disgusting," she told Brew after she had repositioned the pot and washed her hands. "Maybe it's better than battling a blizzard, but not by much."

Brew happily gurgled back at her.

There had to be a better solution, but Kate couldn't come up with anything short of asking Santa Claus. Kate implored any northward-wafting breeze to carry her message to Santa.

Christmas would be there in less than eight weeks. Maybe he would have a flusher on his sled.

Kate hoped she'd be getting her throne soon. And until then, the old privy had been working fine for years. She'd just use that, unless the weather was *really* bad.

But the camp box was perfect for Attie because it was low and there was no need to worry about her falling through into a pit below. So, it could be Attie's to practice on.

Kate had noticed that Attie was such a big girl now, that she liked to climb over the gate and give the camp box a try every once in a while.

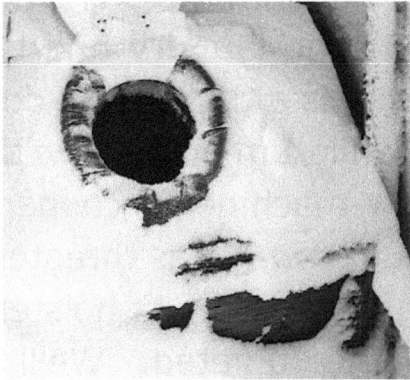

* * *

One evening Tim called from Pump Station One, (where he had been assigned the month before).

"Hi Timber. Yup, we're fine. Attie and I had a little battle of the wills this afternoon. I won—but *barely*. I had to threaten to paddle her with a wooden spoon to get her attention. But she finally told me where she'd hidden Brew's 'Blankie.' They're asleep now, thankfully." Kate paused. "I sure do miss you, Timber."

"I miss you too, babe," Tim said. "My R&R's coming up soon. You just be safe. Stay out of Fram's way 'til I get back."

"We will—and everyone else's too."

"How are you holding up?" Tim asked.

"So far so good. I still hate 'shower day.' Sledding the laundry and the children down to the car is a trick, and I don't want to think about while I'm actually *in* the shower. But the snow-machine is cooperating, and nothing—and *no one*—has threatened us yet, so the shotgun is still in its holster."

Kate's voice quieted. "We'll be waiting for you, Daddy, all healthy and shined up when you get back."

"Good. I'll be home for Christmas." He said and hung up.

And that was that.

* * *

"What's this in the stove?" It was the next morning and Kate had just opened the stove door to start the morning fire. Inside, all of her wooden spoons were leaning together in a little wigwam shape. It looked like a pyre waiting for the match. Clearly, Atwood Peters had implemented her sneaky plan sometime before dawn. Such an ingenious little girl!

Brew was an easy-going boy—but no one had better try to take away his "Blankie," for any reason.

* * *

Thanksgiving came and went with understated flair. The holiday they were waiting for was Christmas. Those next weeks seemed to tick by slowly.

* * *

JOURNAL-DECEMBER 2
WE'VE HAD SOME WARM WEATHER, AND THE
ROAD IS SIX INCHES DEEP WITH MUD ALL THE
WAY DOWN TO WHERE THE CAR IS PARKED.
I HAVE TO BEAT IT HELL-BENT-FOR-LEATHER DOWN
THE TRAIL AT A THIRTY DEGREE ANGLE WHILE
TRYING TO STAY ON ANY SNOW
THAT'S STILL LYING ON THE SHADY SIDE OF
THE ROAD. IT'S A PRETTY HAIRY RIDE WITH
TWO KIDS STRAPPED TO YOU.

Then it got cold again, and the new snow started sticking where it had fallen. After that, traveling home from the car was a pleasure cruise, as long as the snow-machine started and the children stayed content.

All Dressed Up for the Holidays

AS CHRISTMAS APPROACHED, Tim's little family grew more and more excited. Their daddy would be home soon.

"He's been away for so long, he won't even recognize you, Brew," Kate said as she strained to lift her solidly-built boy up and out of his crib.

Attie started skipping down the hall, singing with glee, "Daddy coming home! Daddy coming home!"

Kate was singing, too. She missed Tim's quirky sense of humor and his profound determination. Also, since no one ever visited, she couldn't wait for some adult conversation.

She was ready for a break. Although she had most of the modern conveniences now, she still felt worn out. She'd had her hands full, taking care of the farm and two babies for the last ten weeks.

. . . But Attie wasn't really a baby anymore. She'd already learned to read! They'd been reading a lot together, and the little girl could sound out most of the words in her favorite books. What a smarty! Daddy would be impressed when he saw his darling daughter's newest talent.

* * *

Tim's Christmas R&R eventually did get there, and he was home for two blissful weeks. Kate talked her head off about everything that had happened while he'd been away. Attie bounced on her daddy's knee, and Brew, who had learned to sit up, and liked it, seemed pretty happy tinkering with whatever was within his reach.

* * *

Now it was Christmas Eve. They'd hung colored lights outside, which framed both the front window and the Christmas tree inside. Those beacons stood at the ready, shining out into the dark. They would guide Santa's reindeer directly to the Peterses' smokestack. Little Attie was anxiously awaiting the arrival of "Sanna Cause."

So far, he hadn't come, and excited as the little girl was, both she and Brew were getting sleepy.

A sudden knock on the door startled the foursome from a family-cuddle daze in front of the holiday tree. There hadn't been any snowmobile lights or sounds.

"Who could it be?" Kate asked Tim. "Is it Sanna?" Attie cried, rolling out of her daddy's arms and running to the window to see if the big man was out there. Tim got up and looked through the thick window in the handmade door. There were two cross-country skiers standing outside.

As he opened the door, the skiing jesters broke into song, belting out *Deck the Halls!* This delighted the astonished family and, after the carol, these impromptu visitors were invited inside for some eggnog beside the fire. They stood their skis up in the snow and ascended the steps.

"We saw your Christmas lights from the top of the mountain, and we wanted to wish you a merry Christmas," said the first man. "You have to respect someone who lives way out in the middle of nowhere and still puts up Christmas lights."

The other young man winked at Attie. "Santa won't have any trouble finding *your* house," he told her.

The six had a short, cheerful visit, and then the mystery guests went outside and strapped on their skis, ready to continue their starlit sojourn.

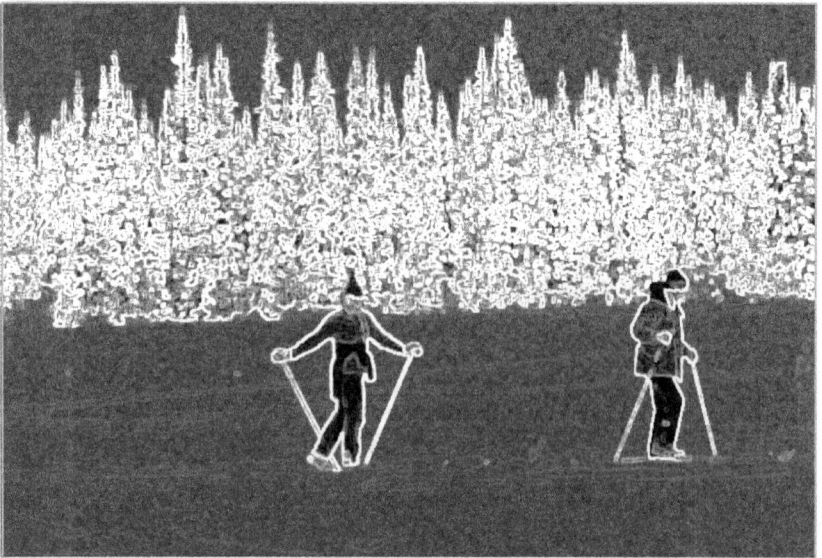

"Gosh, that was a surprise," Kate said, as she watched the strangers glide away.

Then she turned to Attie. "Well, Miss Atwood, since we're so close to the North Pole, Santa will probably be getting here soon, so you'd better hop in the sack. He might be here any minute."

At that, Attie jolted from the window, bolted down the hall, and dove under her covers. Kate followed with a slumbering Brew and softly tucked both sleepy-eyed children into bed.

* * *

The next morning Attie awoke early and started rousting the sleepyheads.

"Kissmuss, Daddy! Kissmuss!" She shook her daddy's hand to wake him.

Both parents dutifully climbed out of bed and grabbed their robes and slippers. Kate got Brew changed while Tim got a fire going, and then they all began studying the festive tree and all that lay beneath.

Santa had been there, all right, and Attie was dazzled by the miracle. She could hardly contain her enthusiasm for the hunt; but Tim wanted to keep the whole family involved in the joyous day, so he told her he would hand out one gift at a time.

"Now let's see what's under this tree," he said, taking on the role of Santa's elf. He handed one gift to each child. "Here you go, Attie. And here's one for you, Brew."

Attie rode her new red riding horse around the room while eight-month-old Brew was content to play with the growing pile of crinkling giftwrap paper beside him.

When the tree was bereft of gifts, Tim told Kate he liked his new moose-hide slippers, while Kate—who still wished there had been a toilet hiding in the corner—claimed to be delighted with the hamburger press Mrs. Claus had sent. Attie and Brew played, and with the exception of one missing item, the four Peterses were content.

With copious cups of cocoa and coffee, it all turned out to be a perfect family day— the kind of Baby's First Christmas that Kate would want to remember forever.

By the end of that perfect day,
both children were tuckered out—but happy!

Washing Machine

AFTER STRUGGLING TO barely keep the home fires burning all that fall, Kate told Tim she wanted to take the children up to Fairbanks and rent an apartment for the rest of that winter and through "breakup." Even *with* running water, living on the mountain was tricky without her handy husband around to keep everything going.

So, after the holidays, they all went north—where Brew and Attie both promptly came down with the chickenpox.

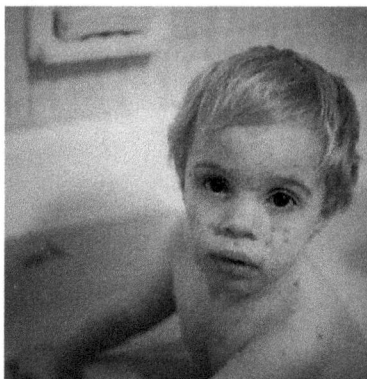

Luckily, their apartment had a bathtub, so the children were able to suffer through their ordeal with long soaks and lots of sherbet.

* * *

Then summer came again, and the Peters family headed home to their mountain. It was a soggy Saturday in mid-June when they arrived at the turnoff in Sleeping Moose. They bumped into and out of mud puddles for the first two miles, as Tim steered up the dirt road. At the bridge they stopped to survey the situation.

It didn't look like anyone was left at Frampton's corner. Relief number one.

Tim parked the Gremlin just before the steep hill to Goodmans' and they all started hoofing it up to the house.

"Here Brew, you're dragging your blanket. Let me carry it for you," his mother offered.

"No," Brew *still* insisted on maintaining control of his blanket at all times.

"Then you'll need to pick it up." It was an impossibly long walk for such a little boy, so Tim picked up his son and started carrying him on his shoulders.

Kate took Attie's hand and started to sing, and the family forged ahead up the mountain.

* * *

Summer, 1983

Greetings from the Mountain, Tutu! We made it through the winter. Heading up to Fairbanks was probably a good idea for us. You know me and machines. Anyway, we're home at last.

Tim is now working two-weeks-on / two-weeks-off, so he can be here a lot more this summer. That'll be much better.

Attie is happy to be home. She likes to show her little brother (who is now walking) all her old toys, and he looks pretty interested. Brew is happy most of the time, as long as I keep him fed. This boy is ravenous and strong.

I'm hoping we can get a washing machine up here this year. Then we'll have almost all the conveniences.

Love Kate, Tim, and the children

* * *

On Tim's first two-weeks-off rotation, he caught Kate looking at the bags of laundry waiting by the door. She wasn't looking excited about the upcoming washhouse excursion.

"What's up?" he asked.

"Oh, I was just thinking about how much I dislike doing the laundry in town."

"You dislike it?"

"Yes. Hauling the laundry into town is a pain. Not to mention showering the kids there."

Tim put up his hands. "Whoa. We're not anywhere *near* ready to put in a shower."

"Oh, I know, darlin'; but yesterday on "Radio Trader" there was a guy in Anchor Point who sells used washers. How hard would it be to hook up a washer, do you think?"

"Not very," Tim said.

Brew and Attie were crawling in and out around their parents' legs, playing some kind of keep-away. Standing was getting tricky.

"But what's wrong with the washer Neil gave you?" he asked, referring to the antique instrument Neil Goodman had pulled out and bequeathed to Kate before heading outside to the Lower Forty-Eight. It resembled a plumber's plunger.

"You agitate by pumping it up and down," Neil had explained. And Kate had figured that it might also unplug a toilet, if she ever had one.

She remembered looking over at Elsie, who'd said, "It works all right, but I don't recommend it."

"That's more of a collector's item," Kate started to explain.

Tim smiled at her and said, "Why don't you go ahead and call the guy and find out how much he's asking?"

"You wouldn't mind?" Kate glowed in this good fortune. "If we could get a washer up here, all my problems would be over."

* * *

That Saturday, when the washer salesman came on to give his pitch, Kate took down his number and called. By the time Tim came back into the kitchen she had a quote for him. "He has some washers for thirty-five-dollars. What do you think? Can we do it?"

Tim shrugged. "I guess we can swing that."

Kate clapped her hands and made up one of her impromptu ditties.

"Oh-Yippee. Oh-Yay!
I get a washer today!"

"Not today," Tim said. "But soon, maybe."

"Okay, I can wait." (After all, she'd been hauling her wash out for the last six years.

She could surely wait a little longer without cracking.)

Bless his heart. The very next Saturday Tim went off to buy a washer for his bride. He took Attie along for company, and Brew and his mom stayed home to play in the garden. "We should be gone about four hours. Five tops," he promised, as he and Attie left.

* * *

The first half of the day had been sunny, but by the early afternoon it had socked in, and now rain had mucked up everything. Brew and his mommy, held captive indoors, sat watching through the window for any sign of their truck coming up the road.

Hours went by. Five hours. Six hours. Where *were* they?

Kate asked her baby boy, "What do you suppose happened to them?"

Brew had no idea how to respond.

"The M-37 doesn't have much in the way of brakes," she went on. "Do you have any idea how many hills there are between here and Anchor Point?"

The one-year-old couldn't imagine.

"And there's that one steep ravine. If the brakes went out on that hill . . ." She cut herself off. "Let's not even think about it."

Brew *already* wasn't thinking about it. He was thinking about lunch—and this lady was his meal ticket. He tried to get his mother to focus on his big blue eyes, but she seemed distracted. The little lad figured if she didn't come up with the goods pretty soon, he'd have to start crying.

He gave one or two warning whimpers, but she was oblivious.

"What if I caused them to crash, just because I thought I needed a washing machine? Brew, if I'm a widow—and your sister and father are dead because *I* asked them to go halfway down the Kenai in a truck with no brakes just so I could have a washer—I'll never forgive myself."

Brew had his own problems. He guessed it was time to start making a scene. He began waving his little fists.

"They should have been home by now." Kate looked at the clock. "It's been over *seven* hours."

A sudden realization evaporated her perseveration. "Good grief! It's *way* past your lunch time! I'm *sorry* Brew. You must be a hungry little guy."

You got that right, Brew agreed telepathically.

Kate put him in his high chair and spoon-fed peas and pears and rice. All the while she kept her eyes on the road, waiting for whatever news would soon be coming to their door.

Another hour went by. Brew had fallen asleep on the couch as his mom sat beside him. He figured if she was smart, she'd follow his example and take a little nap, too. Kate stared out at the field. Brew slept as his mother worried for the both of them.

She was wondering whether they even knew enough people around there to carry two coffins.

* * *

At the tail end of that extra-long summer day—nearly nine hours after Tim and Attie had gone off to fetch the washer— Kate started to hear a faint bumping noise.

Soon it sounded like the M-37 was bouncing up the road. Kate sat upright. "It's your sister and your daddy! They're home!" She rose and rushed to the door. "They're home, Brew, and they've brought us a . . ." But Kate's victory dance trailed off, because she saw no big white box riding in the back.

Two seconds after her relief at their return, she was struck with disappointment.

While she had *truly* been worried for her loved ones, she had also been holding out hope that they'd have a washing machine with them when they got home. It was a dichotomy. Doing her best to curb her incongruous feelings, she spoke to Brew.

"Remember, sweet boy, we're just glad they're home safe," she reminded him. "We didn't really *need* a washer, so don't cry."

Kate watched the truck swing to the left, stop, and start backing up the last fifty feet of driveway.

And that's when she saw that there *was* something big and square in the back of the truck: it just wasn't *white* . . . it was *blue!* There was a robin's-egg-blue washing machine bumping its way up to her house!

"Look, Brew. All that worrying for nothing." More than doubly relieved, the overwhelmed housewife began to cry.

"Sorry we took so long," Tim said when he saw her tears. "There was a guy whose truck was crosswise in the road just this side of Tanners' driveway. I had to pull him out before I could get past. Anyway, here's your washer. I hope you like it."

"Like it? *I love it!*" the delighted and much-relieved housewife exclaimed.

When her daddy dropped the tailgate Attie proudly announced, "I picked it out, Mommy. Blue, for you."

* * *

The next morning, the pair hefted the washer down the steps to the basement. It was astoundingly heavy and awkward, but they managed to get the turquoise lady down unscratched.

"Open the door," Tim panted.

Kate caught the latchstring and gave it a pull.

The basement door was locked.

"Didn't you unlock it this morning?" Tim asked.

"No. Didn't *you?*"

The two teamsters were flummoxed.

Tim assumed Captainship. "One of us will have to go upstairs and come down the interior steps to unlock the door."

"Right."

It was tight at the bottom, with no room to maneuver and no place to set the thing down. The frustrated movers looked around, holding what felt like a ton of tin between them.

There was no alternative. They'd have to muscle the load back up the steps, set it on the truck till the door was unlocked, and then carry it down the stairs all over again.

They lifted it back up the steps and set it partway onto the truck bed. Kate balanced it there while Timmy went in through the upstairs door and raced around to the bottom entrance.

As they wrestled the machine down the stairwell for a second time Kate breathlessly suggested, "Let's learn a lesson from this. Let's have a plan, and then check first, to make sure the path is clear *before* we start moving something heavy. Good idea?"

Tim grunted in agreement.

The team finally got their load delivered to where it was bound, and it certainly did look beautiful sitting there in its newly-designated laundry area. Someday it would be hooked up, Kate had no doubt. She had married the most *able* man in the world.

And how sweet of Attie to pick out her mommy's favorite color. Kate could just imagine the two walking between rows of old washers until Attie saw the one she thought her mommy would love.

"Attie, what would you like for supper tonight?"

"Macaloni and cheese, okay?"

"Okay."

By evening, Kate felt she had learned three very important lessons about washing machines:

1. Don't send your husband off to pick up a washing machine in a truck without brakes unless you're prepared to spend the next portion of your life as a widow.
2. Clear the path *before* you pick up your washing machine!

3. Don't pick up your washing machine if there's anyone around who is willing to do it for you.

* * *

After one concentrated Sunday of laboring in the basement, Tim had the washer hooked up and functioning.

Just as soon as he'd gotten the thing plumbed, he would be headed back north for work. But that was okay.

By Monday noon, Kate was hanging out the first laundry on her line in the back yard. The children were laughing and playing (not fighting, for once) on their swing set, while their mother snapped out lovely-smelling Levi's. The weather was perfect, and Kate was thinking that even if they never got any farther than this, it was a *glorious* spot to be left hanging.

That summer, there was a population explosion on Round Top Mountain. The Radleys had convinced two of their friends to buy parcels from Goodman, which swelled the census of the little end-of-the-road settlement to eight, and that wasn't counting the four Snyders who were still hanging around part-time down at the bridge.

Butch, one of the new landowners, was a fisherman. The other guy, Jason, was a hunting guide and a bush pilot. Kate had hoped they'd have women with them, but they turned out to be bachelors. The two friends planned to build cabins right across the road from each other with their places backing up to the little copse of trees at the high end of Goodman's field. The view would be terrific from there.

Although the neighborhood was filling in, there was still plenty of open space between homesites, and Tim and Kate didn't see much change with the recent influx.

Carl came up to borrow tools and supplies pretty often, but he still didn't have time to stay and chat. And neither of the new guys ever came up at all.

Jillian and Kate had never really hit it off—just different vibes. Hopefully Butch or Jason would be bringing another woman into the enclave someday. In the meantime, when Kate visited with Jillian occasionally, she tried to steer the conversation away from any road issue.

* * *

In mid-summer Carl and Jillian Radley moved up to work on their house full-time, and Jillian put in a little garden near their house site.

At first, things were okay. But one morning, Brew and his mama walked down to pay a call on neighbor J. Radley.

While the two women were talking about recent events on the mountain, Brew innocently waddled over to Jillian's vegetable garden to get a better look at the gigantic rhubarb leaves. He took hold of the wire fence . . . and, *Yeow!*

Kate couldn't believe Jillian had allowed the little toddler to touch an electrified fence without calling out a warning. She ran and grabbed up her stunned baby and hustled him home, thinking they might not return until Brew was at least a teenager. The episode left her with sour feelings toward her neighbor, although that was probably nothing compared to Brew's confusion.

* * *

When fall arrived that year, everyone left the mountain. Carl and Jillian went back to Anchorage, and the Peters family decided to go back to Fairbanks, where Kate was happiest while Tim was away working.

Both the fisherman and the guide disappeared into their winter playgrounds, and Frampton may or may not have stayed where he was. No one claimed to know what made *that* guy tick.

Landing Lights for Santa

"IF THE RAINDEERS   can't get here, how will Santa come?   Will he be on a snow mushing?"

It was Christmas Eve, and Attie was concerned over logistics. The family had come down to share an old-fashioned Christmas on the mountain. Now, a minor blizzard had blown in. Would Santa miss their landing lights? Naturally the little girl was worried about his finding, and then landing on their remote and isolated roof. She'd been looking outside for signs of the jolly old elf for nearly a minute, and her nose had formed a circle of frosted fog on the windowpane.

"I'm sure he's used to weather like this," her mommy said. "He lives up at the North Pole. And *that* means he'll

101

probably be stopping here before he goes down south. So, we'd better all hop into bed now. He'll be here soon."

Attie gave a yelp, flew down the hall, and excitedly climbed up to her new top bunk.

Brew, not yet grasping the great significance of Christmas, dawdled behind.

Kate tucked both children into bed, sat and read aloud their favorite Christmas poem, kissed them each good-night, and left them with sugar plums dancing in their heads.

* * *

"Daddy, get up! Mommy, get up!" Attie was shaking them awake. "Santa was here!"

Kate sat up and hugged her little girl. "Good old Santa. I knew he'd make it." She got up, got Brew out of his crib, and followed Attie down the hall to see what old St. Nicholas had left behind.

There was a lot of stuff under the tree, but no toilet that Kate could see. If it was there, then he'd hidden it well.

"I really hope there's a toilet under here somewhere," she whispered to little Brew.

Tim headed across the room and bent down to look closely at the tree. "Gosh, I see a present for Attie!" He grasped a box. "And here's something for you, Brew," he said, grabbing up a second festooned mystery. He put the gifts into eager little hands.

Then he bent down and scooped up something wrapped in bright green and maroon moose paper. "And here's what Santa brought for you, Mama," Tim said as he handed the shoebox sized gift to Kate.

The green-and-maroon moosed woman grew excited.

Was it a float valve? That would be something small, to represent the magnificent item that was probably sitting outside in the shop at this very moment.

She played along. "Now what is this?"

"Mrs. Claus told me you needed one. She said no home should be without it."

"She did, eh?" Kate figured Mrs. Claus knew plenty about outhouses in the Arctic.

"Open it," Tim prompted.

She opened the box.

Inside was a handle with what looked like a flexible syringe needle protruding from it. Even as she held it in her hands, she still didn't understand what it was used for. "What is it?"

"It's an internal egg-scrambler."

"What do you do with it?"

"With this thing you can scramble your eggs without even breaking them."

"How are you supposed to cook it?"

"Well, then you have to break the shell, I guess."

"Okay, and tell me again, why would you want to scramble your egg before you break the shell?"

"I don't know; maybe to impress your guests at a fancy brunch? Anyway, Mrs. Claus said you'd like it."

"Well, tell her thanks. The next time I host a fancy brunch, I'll be sure to use it."

"Here," Tim said, turning to Attie. He handed his little girl her second box. It had pictures of candy canes all over it. "Can you count the candy canes?"

She got all the way to five before she started tearing the paper off. Inside she found a beautiful plastic golden Palomino horse. "I love you, horsey!" the delighted girl squealed, and she walked it around and pretended that it was nibbling at wrapping paper scraps.

The unveilings continued smoothly until, a half-hour later the room was buried in multicolor wads of paper, and both children were surrounded by toys. The family had completed their excavation of hidden goodies from under the tree.

Kate had looked all around but had found no commode left behind.

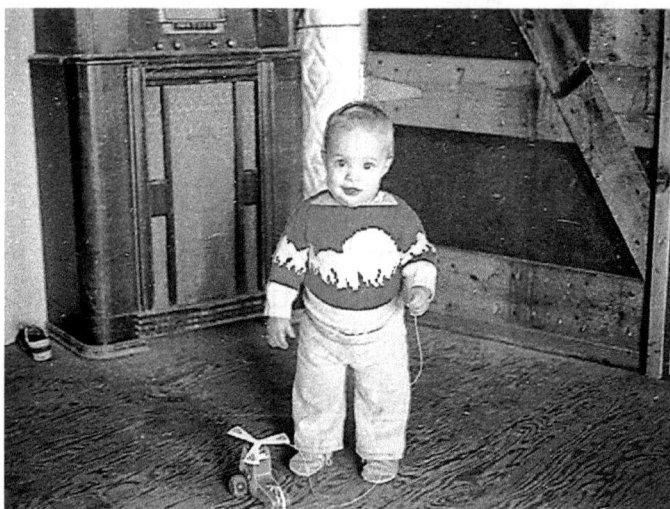

Brew got a little helicopter pull-toy that he quickly took to pulling along behind him wherever he went.

"You look disappointed Kate," Tim said. "Don't you like the egg scrambler Santa brought you?"

"Gosh. I *do* love it. Please thank the Clauses for their suggestions." She paused. "But while you were consulting with them, did you happen to ask about a toilet? No home should be without one of those, either."

Tim was perplexed. "You already have a great little camp-can, back there in the orange room. Do you really need a toilet?"

Kate mentally re-experienced the stench of her most recent emptying ordeal. "Darling, I just want to be able to go to the bathroom, *flush* it, and *never* see it again. That's all."

There. She'd played her trump card. Exasperated, Tim continued rummaging for unopened gifts. But there were none.

The next day Kate paused from doing dishes to watch her family at play through the window. The three of them were building a snowman. The sun glistening on the iced alder branches had turned their world into a crystalline candy land. It was beautiful. Could anything be more perfect?

Maybe the smell of hot cocoa simmering on the stove could make this moment just a little bit sweeter. Soon, the chocolate would be sending its aroma floating across the room, where the scent would linger like a magnet and welcome them inside when they came home with red noses and pink cheeks.

Years before, when they were hewing the timbers for the house, Kate had saved the butt ends of several beams and had made fireside stools out of them. She'd rounded the sharp edges and painted them with log oil.

When her loved ones came in all cold and ebullient, they could sit around the fire and sip hot chocolate, creating a collective memory of family happiness for all time.

* * *

A few days later they headed back to Fairbanks for the remainder of the winter.

Real Kid Stuff

IT WAS DURING the next summer that the Peters children got initiated into *real* kid stuff. That came about when John and Melanie Read purchased a parcel and started building a house on the other side of the big alder patch. They had twin boys, Benny and Bobby, who were almost seven, and *they knew everything*. Attie and Brew soon fell in behind them.

"Let's build a tree house," the twins suggested one morning.

"Okay," Attie said.

"Okay," Brew echoed.

The three older kids evaporated into the woods and little Brew galloped as fast as he could behind them. The four weren't heard from again until they surfaced for lunch— and to borrow a handsaw and some nails and a hammer from Tim.

"What are you doing?" Tim asked, as he filled the tool request list.

"We're building a tree house," Benny said.

"Yeah. It's gonna be really high." Attie announced sounding very excited.

"Really high?"

"Uh-huh. It's way up in the sky."

Tim was glad that he happened to be home while this project was under construction. Maybe he should take a look. "Would you like to show me?"

"Sure." The children happily obliged and led him down through the woods to their chosen site. It was a grove of four strong spruce trees with heavy branches stair-stepping in a spiral upwards maybe ten feet or less. Tim looked it over, and then gave it his approval.

"Looks good, kids. You be careful, now. Don't stand underneath any tools. Always hold on with at least one hand. And watch out for Brew." Then their doting father resolutely turned his back and left them free to grow.

"What does it look like?" Kate asked when Tim got back.

"To a kid, it looks like heaven."

"Not too high?"

"Not *too* high, just high enough. I think they'll be fine. After all, that's why we're out here, isn't it—so the kids can have a perfect childhood?"

"Yes. That's exactly why we're here. But it's still scary. What if they fall?"

"Then we'll patch 'em up. They have to learn, Kate."

"You're right." The mother tucked her concerns away as best she could. "They'll be hungry when they come home."

"So, it's good that John and Melanie moved their family up this year," Tim said. "It'll be nice to have a couple of youngsters on the hill to play with our two."

Kate had already thought about it and had decided that it would be worth giving up her nude gardening to have playmates for her children. "Uh-huh. They seem like nice boys. I think I'm gonna like Melanie, too. She told me she used to dance ballet when she was younger, so we have that in common. It'll be nice to have another family close by."

The tree house took about a week to complete. Benny and Bobby and Attie worked on it almost constantly, while Brew, abandoned at the tree's base, sucked his thumb and watched the bigger kids construct their dream home. He fully intended to join them as soon as he'd mastered the art of climbing that tree.

* * *

The next time Attie asked her daddy to help with their construction project, Tim was happy to oblige.

"Sure. What are you building today?"

"A zipline," Attie said.

"A zipline? Who's got a zipline?" her daddy asked.

"Benny and Bobby. Their daddy is helping us, and maybe you can too."

"Okay," Tim agreed. "Let's go look at what you've got."

Later, when Tim came into the kitchen, he told Kate about the zipline, and she went into a tizzy. "That doesn't sound safe to me. What if somebody falls?"

"Leave them be, Kate, my dear."

"But Brew is too young to be riding a zipline. He's gonna fall."

"Let him be a big boy," his father advised.

"It's hard," Kate said.

The tree house "Gang of Four" had daring fun that August, sliding down the zipline, battling with wooden swords, and exploring the alder patch that grew between their two houses.

Benny taught them all how to make a trap. He dug a steep-sided hole and covered it with grass. The next day there were two mice trapped in the bottom of the pit. One was limping, and Brew immediately devoted himself to its rescue and recovery.

"Mommy, can you fix it?" He had the little mouse cupped in his hands.

"Oh my, honey, I don't think I can, poor little thing. But he lives outside, not inside. You need to take him out now."

"But he's hurt."

"I think he'll make it, if we just let him be. Take him outside and set him down in the shade. If you want to, you can put some water in a jar lid for him. By morning he'll be all better."

"But where's his mommy?"

"Sweetie, he'll be okay. You need to take him outside now, because if he gets loose in here, we'll have to kill him."

"No!" Brew was horrified. Shaking his head, he turned and carried the little mouse back outside, even though he really wanted to nurse the wild creature back to health.

What a sweet little heart!

* * *

One perfect day melted into another, until the summer was nearly over and it was time for the Peters family to head back north. Attie would be starting kindergarten, and they'd need to find a place to spend the winter.

Anna Tanner, who lived farther down the road, also had two children and suggested that Kate could home-school.

Kate shook her head. "We're both too high-strung, and the winters have enough drama by themselves without adding a frustrated schoolmarm and a strong-willed pupil to the mix." So, it was off to Fairbanks at the end of the summer.

But when they got to their winter stomping grounds, there weren't any vacant houses or apartments for rent. Oil was booming, and everyone in the world had come up north looking for work.

Kate and Tim decided to try Anchorage. The situation was the same in that much bigger city by the sea. But construction was booming in Anchorage, and condos were shooting up everywhere. The Peterses had to be settled somewhere before school started. Desperate, Tim and Kate decided to buy a modest condo in a new development.

"This plan looks nice," Kate said. "It's got plenty of sunlight coming in through that big southern window."

"Do you think you and the kids will be happy here while I'm away on the Slope?"

"It has a toilet, right?"

. . . And so, they bought it.

* * *

Later that fall, someone built a three-story complex directly in front of their window, which plunged their city-dwelling into perpetual shade. Kate, frozen-in at home with a preschooler, was quite distressed when the developer broke his promise of a greenbelt and a playground in front, and built a tall wall instead.

A valuable lesson learned.

Buy your sunshine and your view.

−3−

The Golden Years of Camelot

Weasel Tracks

THEY HAD JUST arrived at the house, ready to share almost two whole weeks of Christmas fun at Victory Garden.

"Hey, babe, look at this."

Tim held out the paper they'd picked up in Anchorage.

"What do you want me to see?" Kate was sitting on the fire-tender's beam-butt stool, lighting a fire.

"This." Tim read aloud to her. "1945 Weasel track vehicle. Unbeatable for off-road use. A hunter's dream. $1500.00."

"What's a Weasel?"

"It's a lot like the armored personnel carrier we rode in when I was in Nam. This thing would be able to get us up here, no matter what the conditions."

"Like a tank?"

"Yeah. Pretty much. What say I go take a look at it?"

"Sure. It'd be great, especially if I can start it and steer it. That will be your Christmas present, dear."

"Okay. Good. I'll call the guy right now, and maybe go up to Moose Pass and look at it tomorrow."

Tim called the number, and within a few minutes he was planning his expedition to Moose Pass. "I might as well take the trailer, just in case."

"That sounds like a good idea. Just keep in mind that I'm not handy when it comes to mechanical things."

"Don't worry. You'll love driving this baby."

"Okay, Papa," Kate said. "You go, and the kids and I will stay here and get this place whipped into shape for Santa's big arrival."

Early the next morning Tim drove off in the M-37 with the old flatbed trailer behind.

* * *

BILL OF SALE

In consideration of $1,500 paid to me in hand by ████████, the receipt of which is here-by acknowledged, I, ████, by these present, do bargain, sell and convey to the said ████████, one Weasel and utility trailer, as is, serial number unknown and motor number unknown. I will warrant the said Weasel unto ████ against any lawful claims and demands of all and every person or persons whomever.

He was home by ten that night, hauling a boxy-looking track-vehicle on the straining trailer. Kate went out to look at the newest family addition.

"This should absolutely take care of all our problems with the road," Tim said. He was beaming. "Let's see, we now have three snow-machines, two sleds, an M-37, a Gremlin, two trailers, two sets of cross-country skis, two sets of snowshoes, and a Weasel. That should just about do it."

"I certainly *hope* so. We don't have room to park any more vehicles on this forty-acre lot."

"No. I guarantee we'll be able to get in and get out in *any* weather now."

Kate walked around the load, looking at the metal tracks and the plywood top. It looked like something between a tank and a stagecoach. Kate actually liked the looks of the rig. It had a silly mustache painted on the front—like their truck had. It was just odd looking, like a Citroen car. She smiled. Was there anything *not* to like about it? She didn't think so.

"Well, what do you think of her?" Tim was waiting for her assessment.

"I like her looks. We'll have to see how she performs in the mud, next breakup—and how well I can handle her."

"You're gonna love this thing." Tim was excited. "Tomorrow we'll take the whole family exploring back behind the house. Maybe go up to the top of the mountain."

"That sounds like fun. I'll pack a lunch."

The M-29 Weasel had belonged to a hunter before Tim got hold of it. That guy had made it into a moose hunter's dream when he attached a camouflaged plywood box on top of the old metal frame. A guy and his buddies could sit inside all warmish and cozy, waiting for a moose to wander by, and maybe even shoot it right out through the window. Then they could throw it up on top and transport it home. This same box also made it the perfect family off-road vehicle: a station wagon on tracks.

"Where are the doors?" Kate wanted to know.

"It doesn't have doors. You climb in through the windows."

Kate looked inside. There were no seats either, but the former owner had left six milk crates behind. "Box seating for six." Kate praised, "It looks great, partner. You did good."

* * *

The next morning, they packed some food and water, and the shotgun, and rounded up the kids for a little adventure trip to the summit of Round Top. Tim showed them all how to climb in. "You put your foot on this flat ledge here, and hoist yourself in."

"Good thing we're all young," Kate joked. "All right, kids, in we go." She loaded

Attie and Brew in through the window. Then she climbed up behind them. After trying unsuccessfully to go inside head first, Kate swiveled on the top step and backed in.

Once she was seated on one of the crates, Tim flipped the ignition switch and engaged the starter. Then he pointed out all the operational parts of their new machine.

"This is the clutch, and here's the gas," he said. He took hold of dual steering levers that reminded Kate of a cable car in San Francisco. "You pull this lever and push that one to turn right, and do the reverse to turn left," he said, as he demonstrated. Under his hand the noisy crawler made a complete pivot. "Be careful, though," he warned. "If you swivel too fast, you can throw a track."

"Where's the brake?" Kate's second question.

"There is no brake. When you take your foot off the gas, you'll coast to a stop pretty quick. It's on footprints, not wheels."

Footprints? No brakes? This thing was a mechanical Sasquatch.

Tim told everyone to sit down and hold on. Then he shifted the strange machine into gear, and it lurched forward. The kids laughed, and Kate held onto them to keep them from flying off their crates. When the passenger carrier eventually got its stride, it actually began to dip forward and back, like a buckboard wagon, which delighted Kate. "It feels like we're in a stagecoach, which fits into my western fantasy."

As soon as their mother loosened her grip on their shirtsleeves, both children jumped to the open windows and hung their faces out, overflowing with great expectations. "Whee!" they cried.

The Peters family chugged up the hill and dove straight into the heart of an alder thicket. The tracks began to make "footprints" as Tim guided them between the gnarl of twisted and intertwined alder saplings. Sometimes the machine rose up and bumped down over a low-hanging alder branch.

"Hold on!" Tim finally warned.

The ride was getting exciting. *Even a little too exciting maybe,* Kate thought.

It was so noisy inside the hollow metal box that Tim couldn't hear Kate when she asked if the vehicle was likely to be tippy.

"What?"

"I asked if it's *tippy?* Are we *top* heavy?"

"Nah. A Weasel is *made* for this kind of country."

Tim sounded so confident that Kate tried to ignore the fact that their sideways tilt was getting steeper. Nervous, she reined the children in, just in case. "Attie and Brew, you need to come and sit down."

"We want to ride here," Attie spoke for Brew.

"You need to sit down now," Kate insisted.

The children obeyed—which was good—because the moment they were safely back in her hands, the whole machine tipped sideways at an alarming angle, and anything that was loose flew down to the low side. Both children shrieked.

"Okay," Tim admitted. "Maybe it's time to try a different route."

"Or maybe we should just turn around and head home?"

"I still think we can make it. Let's try over there." The man's spirit of exploration was unquenchable.

They tried several times to punch their way through the untamed alder, but each attempt was thwarted. Finally, Tim had to concede that their own back yard was no Sunday picnic, even in a Weasel.

"Okay, let's go back," he finally agreed.

"That sounds good to me." Kate said, relieved. "But maybe we can go for a spin around the field before we head home. I like riding in this thing."

"Yeah, Daddy. Let's go!" Attie started bouncing up and down, and Brew followed her lead.

"Okay, then. Everybody hold on!" The operator put a hand on each steering lever and moved them in opposition. That spun the Weasel around, and soon they had cleared the tangle of trees and were rolling back out onto the snowy plain.

Tim opened up the throttle and made a set of matching tracks that swept past the front steps and down through the field all the way to the woods below. Then he turned right and rocked the family around their big open front yard. On the way back, Tim changed places with Kate, and she drove the last lap home.

"There. See? It's not hard at all."

"No. It's kind of fun," said the mechanic's wife. But she still wondered how she would handle the thing on her own, if she ever had to.

Christmas of the Matching Sleds

"LET'S GO, DADDY! Let's go!" Attie was tugging at Tim's sleeve. "Let's go get the tree!"

It was the next morning, and Attie and Brew were eager to find the perfect tree for Christmas. Tim was drinking morning coffee with Kate.

"Come on, Daddy!" Attie was standing there with snowsuit in hand and Brew was stomping around in his daddy's huge marshmallow-shaped "bunny boots."

"Okay. Let's go find a tree." Tim got his hatchet and hat, and hooked up the sled. Then he and Attie climbed on the double-track with the sled, and Kate and Brew (now in his own footwear) mounted the single track; and the four rode off on an old-fashioned search for the perfect evergreen.

They found a beauty down in the flat close to Moose Creek. Tim chopped it down and the family sledded it home.

They had hot cider and cookies and then set to work standing up the tree. After they got it all set up in the living room and had it decorated with strings of popcorn and colored lights, the place really looked, sounded, smelled, tasted, and *felt* like Christmas.

"Okay, one more story and then, everyone off to bed."

Everyone went to bed early that evening. In the morning they were going to Soldotna to pick up Grandma Tutu at the airport. She had happily accepted their invitation to an Alaskan bush holiday and said she would be excited to sleep in Honeymoon Cottage. It would be her very own log cabin in the woods.

Christmas morning was perfect.

On Christmas eve Santa came and dropped off matching sleds for the children. The Weasel tracks Tim had etched across the field on their earlier outing made a parallel set of sled runs all the way down to the woods. And they were exactly the right size for the matching sleds Santa had brought.

Attie and Brew spent all Christmas afternoon sledding side-by-side down their fabulous tobogganing race course.

* * *

"Let's go, Daddy!"

This time, it was *sledding* the children were begging for. It was the day after Christmas, and Attie and Brew wanted to demonstrate their newly acquired expertise. Tim, Kate, and Grandma Tutu were still lounging, drinking their morning coffee, and enjoying the view.

"You two go ahead," Tim urged. "Just stay in the tracks we made the other day and see if you can get all the way to the woods without stopping."

"But we want you to watch," Attie countered.

"We'll watch from the window. You two go ahead."

"Please come, Daddy."

They looked like little Michelin men, totally muffled from head to foot in fiberfill and boots. And their shining smiles were irresistible. "Okay. You go start, and I'll be out in a minute."

They ran outside, leaving the adults alone. Tim and Kate held hands for a minute, happy to be watching their children being children.

Then, Tim suited up and went out, intent upon starting a snowball fight.

Kate watched the game from her view chair for a couple of minutes, and then she slapped her thighs. "I think I'll go out for a quick snowshoe sojourn. Do you mind being left alone for awhile, Mamasan?"

"Of course not. You go ahead. I might even go out and join their fun."

Kate saw the happy twinkle in her mother's eye and needed no more encouragement. She rose, put on a wool sweater and a hat, and took her snowshoes down off their nails. Stepping outside, the young mother quietly buckled on her Bear Paws as snowballs whizzed past. She was headed for the solitude of the trees.

When she got to her favorite spruce grove, Kate turned and looked back at her family playing and laughing in the sunshine. Eternally young Grandma Tutu had come outside to observe the Arctic antics of her grandchildren, and she looked like she was having fun.

Kate thought about those years in Hawaii. There had been no snowball fights in her youth. That's partly why she had come here. Now, she felt contentment. In a whimsical mood, she crooned a spontaneous "Winnie-the-Pooh" style ditty to herself.

"What a wonderful, wonderful spot to be.
Oh lucky, lucky, lucky me!"

Then she ducked into the cathedral-like cluster of spruce and began to search for new and interesting things to see. By the time she returned to the house—carrying a strikingly elegant owl feather of perfect contours—Kate was completely revitalized.

Once inside, she hung her snowshoes, hat, and sweater in the warming area, checked the fire and then put on water for hot chocolate. The group outside would love to have nice, warm, chocolate drinks waiting when they were done playing.

After a while, the happy snowball-fighting sledders got cold and came inside to warm up by the wood stove.

"Yum! I smell chocolate," Attie cried, as soon as Kate began stirring the heated water into mugs filled with sweet cocoa powder.

The Peters children shed their outer gear and took seats on beam-butt stools. Tim took the recliner and Tutu sat on the couch.

Kate brought over mugs of hot cocoa and handed them to her four most favorite people. As they warmed their hands with fingers cupping their mugs, she made a toast. "I hope we'll never forget this wonderful Christmas and this perfect year we've had here on the mountain."

"I certainly won't ever forget this special week," Grandma Tutu assured her daughter.

"We won't forget, either" Attie and Brew pledged. Tim nodded, and they all raised a mug to 1984.

* * *

Dear Mamasan,

I guess you're back home in the tropical sunshine now. It was so wonderful to have you spend the holidays with us.

You looked ebullient and lovely, especially when you climbed up into the Weasel, as gracefully as a circus star.

I love you! Kate

Kate Has a Hopper

ON NEW YEAR'S day, the family had to head back to the city and right after they got to Anchorage Tim left for Prudhoe Bay. The Peterses' dream-world existence was on hold again until Easter.

Tim's job schedule soon changed, and now he would be home one week out of every month. This new three-weeks-on / one-off schedule worked out a lot better for Kate, who was feeling like a woman stranded in a dark condo with two small children. Now she could get a little relief every twenty-one days—whether she needed it or not.

In January, Kate's birthday came along and she turned thirty-five. Tim wanted to come up with the perfect gift for her; but what did you give a girl who had everything?

That morning Kate stretched, got up, and went out to put on the coffee. There it was, sitting in the living room, all shiny and new, with balloons sticking up out of it. A hopper! Kate skipped back into the bedroom and dove onto the sleeping man. "Oh Timber! A toilet! Thank you. Thank you. *Thank you!*

"They didn't have turquoise, so I got white," Tim said. "Is that okay?"

"It's *very* okay. You can be absolutely sure of that. It's the most beautiful birthday present I've ever received!

"Anything to keep my little wife happy," Tim said with a smile.

"Believe me, your wife is *very* happy!" And that was the absolute truth.

That toilet bowl was Kate's favorite present, ever.

The Most Endearing Easter

"ARE WE THERE yet?" Attie was asking again.

"Soon. Just a couple more miles," her parents assured her. "We're close."

It had been no surprise that they'd had to park the Gremlin down at the bridge, and the children were doing their best to walk up the mountain without too much complaining. But the trek through knee-deep snow was taking its toll on the little ones. When they began to droop—and finally dragged to a stop altogether—Tim had a brainstorm. "Why don't you three wait right here, while I go get the Weasel?"

"Yay, Daddy!" both children were overjoyed and Kate joined in, too. "Ya-hoo!"

"That sounds great," she added, as she searched out a fallen tree nearby and and sat down. She and the children could sit there and wait for a taxi. Her darlings plopped down on either side of their mother and laid their heads on her lap. Attie, Brew, and Kate would be happy to rest and wait for him to return with some form of transportation.

Tim took off solo, probably glad to be able to speed up to his natural gait. He quickly disappeared around the bend.

The little ones were pooped, and they both sagged against their mama's thighs for the first minute or two. But when a territorial battle erupted and they started pushing each other off the coveted center of her lap, Kate kicked them both off and told them to go find some forest treasures. In short order, they were happily exploring together.

Kate watched over them and sang pretty tunes, both to entertain and to protect her cubs from any other mother and cubs that might be out and about that spring.

When she finally began to hear the clanking sounds of the Peterses' newest rig coming down the road, Kate rounded up the children and held them tight until Tim and the mechanized box had lurched their way to a stop.

Once the machine was safely in idle, Tim poked his head out the side window and smiled down at his family. "Welcome aboard," he said with a jolly salute.

The children saluted back.

Since they weren't carrying much in the way of supplies—just enough food for the week—Tim kept his hands on the controls while Attie clambered up and into the bus. Next, Kate shoved two bags of groceries inside. She boosted Brew up to the window and then she climbed up onto the track, and backed in through the window, one-leg-at-a-time, as gracefully as a ballerina.

Once the groceries were settled and the children were seated, she gave Tim the "go-ahead." She'd hold onto her little ones' squirming parka ruffs and keep them seated until it was safe to stand.

Tim spun the vintage M-29 around and took his family up to the home he had built for them with his own two hands. He deserved proud.

* * *

By the time they got home, it was too late in the day for sledding. Kate built a fire and told Attie she could turn on the TV, take a blanket, and curl up on the couch until the chill was out of the place. Brew quickly followed suit.

Both youngsters struck zombie-like poses and watched one piece of meaningless drivel after another while the room gradually warmed. Kate let them snuggle under their lap rugs until supper time. They were so tired and it was still cold.

They had a hot supper and then it was off to their beds where the sheets were icy and there was no TV. The kids explained all this and begged to come back out and watch more TV under blankets by the fire, but they lost that appeal. When it came to silly sitcom shows with canned laughter, Kate was admittedly a snob.

Soon they were both asleep, without too much harm having been done to their brains.

$$* * *$$

The next morning both youngsters stationed themselves in front of the television as soon as they got up. Evidently, they were planning on a full day of nothingness. Since this wasn't what their parents had envisioned as a wilderness family holiday, Kate fed them oatmeal and then started herding them toward the door.

"Why don't you two go sledding? It's a nice sunny day."

"We want to watch TV."

"You can watch TV up in the city. Maybe you can do a bit of exploring out in the alder."

"We'd rather watch TV," Attie said again. They looked like they were digging in.

Setting her feet a little further apart and putting her hands on her hips, their mother explained the lengths to which she and their father had gone in order to provide them with their fantastic front yard, which they were ignoring. "There's a wonderful, wild world right outside that door, just waiting for you two to discover it."

They weren't listening.

"Most kids will never get to see this."

Nothing registering.

"Do you two realize how lucky you are?"

No reaction.

Kate's voice grew shrill as her patience unraveled. "The challenges here have been *huge*. Maybe you children need to start understanding that, right now! Yesterday, do you remember how hard it was walking all that way up in the snow? And then your daddy went and got the Weasel? . . . How many of your friends have ever ridden home in a Weasel, Attie?"

The children looked up at her. *Was she talking to them?*

"If all you two want to do is watch TV, then we might as well have stayed in the city. But since we *have* provided you with this wonderful place, you're darned-well gonna get out there and enjoy *it. Now move it, both of you!"* Since she was shouting by this time, the youngsters finally realized that she *was* talking to them.

Attie started to whine. "If you make us go outside, that means you don't love us."

"Yes, that's right. You guessed it. Now out you go."

"Just one more show. Puh-leeze? It's Brew's favorite."

"Puh-leeeeeeze?"

"No!" Kate's voice exploded like a boiling tomato. With record strides she roared over to the TV and snapped it off. Then she grabbed their snowsuits out of the warming closet and threw them onto the floor in front of two startled children.

"No more TV until you've both been outside for at least an hour."

And out they went.

* * *

Once she got them out the door, they never came in till lunch. Then they wanted to go right back out till supper. They found a thousand things to do out there in the snow that day, including sledding and snow fort-building, and tracking little animals. When they finally *did* come in, their mother sat them in a warm bath, and gave them each a wash cloth "porpoise" to swim with.

"This is my favorite place in the whole world, Mommy," Attie said.

"Good, dear. I'm glad you had fun."

"Can we play outside again tomorrow?"

"Yes."

"Goody!"

"Goody!" Brew echoed his big sister, and then he splashed his terry cloth porpoise with immense approval and delight.

The children slept like marathoners that night, and when they arose, they couldn't wait to get back outside.

Kate and Tim didn't see much of the kids the next day. And they saw no neighbors or recreationing townspeople at all during that whole *week*.

Since the Reads had taken the twins "outside" to visit relatives, and the Radleys hadn't come down from Anchorage, and Butch and Jason weren't around either, that week turned out to be the most endearing Easter *ever* for the Peterses. It was filled with the kind of specialness that *almost* made up for the excruciating effort it took to be there.

. . . Then it was back to the city, for another three months of the blues.

*That Tesoro gas station was always good to see
on the dark winter road.*

* * *

In mid-June breakup was over and their annual migration south had finally come.

The road around Turnagain Arm and over the Chugach mountains seemed to take an eternity and there were lots of pit stops. Dear Tim obliged his family's needs as graciously as any man who was heading for a destination could.

No one was around when they got to Fram's corner. Kate took this as a good sign. Maybe the Snyders had *finally* left.

Tim parked the car at a wide spot just above the bridge, and the little family started hiking the last four miles up the hill.

* * *

"How much more?" little Attie whined.

They had already walked most of the way.

"We're almost there. It's just around that bend."

The children hiked the last fifty yards through the trees and burst out at the base of their front meadow.

"I see it!" Attie shouted. "Come on, Brew!" She sprinted ahead and Brew broke into a fast waddle, doing his best to keep up.

"Well, babe, this is it," Tim said as he and Kate watched their two children race the last two hundred yards home. "This year the kids are big enough to enjoy the place."

"Uh-huh, this really *is* it. This is what we've worked so long and so hard for," Kate agreed.

The two pioneers stood admiring their family treasure as it gleamed in rays of late-afternoon sunshine. The shining path of light bathed Victory Garden in a warm glow.

They were home.

Over there was Honeymoon Cottage, smiling for them and stretching up her neck like a well-loved pet tortoise.

They walked up the dirt road through purple pompons and golden sun and finally stood at their front door. Kate thought of that day when they'd installed it. "I remember the day we put this door in," she said.

"If anyone else was around, they'll remember it, too," Tim laughed.

"Ah, but that was the beauty back then," Kate reminisced. "No one else *was* around. We could've built this *whole house* in the nude, if we'd a-wanted to."

"Wait a minute," Tim reminded her. "What about when Brian came up that time?"

"One visitor in a half-dozen years? I'll take those odds." She grew serious. "To be honest, I liked it better back then."

"Me too, but I guess those days are gone, babe."

Tim took his mate's hand and urged her forward, picking up their pace. "Hey, come on. It's still the most beautiful spot I know. Let's make the most of this summer and hope that peace will prevail in the neighborhood."

"That would be nice," Kate said. "Let's hope."

* * *

Most of the summer did pass smoothly, due to minimal interaction between the Peterses and everyone else on their road.

Tim came down on weekends, and Kate gardened, and the children played. No one came by, except Jillian who was up once to discuss a plan to get the commuter plane flight pattern changed. She said she didn't like the planes flying overhead.

Kate thought this was a ridiculous idea. In fact, for years she had looked *forward* to seeing the fourteen-seater fly past every morning. Waving to the pilot and passengers was practically her only connection with the outside world.

Kate didn't want to complain about her winged friends, and her momentary pause told Jillian all she needed to know.

Jillian turned and walked back down the hill in a poorly-disguised huff, which was fine with Kate. She loved the planes, and she continued to wave at them every morning that whole summer.

Rare Visitors Well-Done

NOT ON THE road to anywhere at all, they seldom had visitors. And Jillian didn't come up much anymore, so on balmy days Kate decided it would be safe to take advantage of their solitude and try gardening in the buff.

This was a balmy day. Kate was steering a loaded wheelbarrow packed with compost around and in between her wildflower circles circles.

She stopped to rest for a moment.

The Flower Child farmer—dressed in nothing but a hat and boots—set down the barrow's handles, stretched out her back, and gazed absently over across the meadow.

There were two people walking up the road. Who's this? Kate abandoned her task and ducked inside the house. "Hey, Timber, we've got hikers coming up the road!" she announced, stepping inside.

Tim went out to take a look. He made a quick study of the approaching party and then popped his head back in the door. "It looks like Dick and Bob. I'll go meet 'em."

Tim went down the hill to meet up with his old friends and Kate hustled to put on some clothes. By the time the trio got to the door she was all covered and composed.

Dick explained that he'd brought Bob up to show him the hunting grounds behind Tim and Kate's place.

"Where'd you leave your car?"

"My camper van couldn't make it up your road," Bob said. "We walked in from below the bridge. Saw your neighbor hanging around. Do I need to worry?"

"Let's take the M-37 and go get your rig," Tim said. "Kate, do you want to come?"

"No. That's okay," she said. "Getting cars stuck and unstuck is more *men's* fun."

As soon as the three fellows took off down the road, Kate started thinking about what she could offer them for supper.

She looked around the half-finished kitchen and her eye fell on the brown metal box with a glass door that Tim had recently brought home from a garage sale.

The used appliance took up a lot of valuable space on her counter. It had better be something special to warrant such a big slice of kitchen real estate. Time to try it out and see what a*Radar-Range* could do.

The young cook went downstairs and got a roast out of the freezer. Those Goodmans had really done them a favor when they sold the freezer with all the steaks and roasts still inside. Would Elsie be shocked to know Kate was planning to use atomic rays instead of the oven to cook the meat? Probably.

Eventually the three men returned, towing Bob's bus up the hill. They all looked muddy and happy as they trooped inside to open the first "Mickey's Big Mouth" of the day.

After a second beer, Tim walked them up to the windbreak and pointed out the bear trail that took off from there.

The rest of the afternoon would be devoted to beer drinking and catching up on old times.

Several beers later, Kate decided it was time to try out her new countertop-cooking thingy.

She unwrapped the thick leg of beef, set it on a plate in the microwave-sender device, and set the timer for fifteen minutes.

Ding.

When the little bell rang, she went to check on the roast. No change. Repeating her steps, this time she doubled the time.

Ding.

There was still no change in color or aroma. The meat wasn't even defrosted yet! Cooking supper was starting to look like it might take longer than she'd planned.

She worked at that roast for another four hours, while they all drank beers and swapped stories. Finally, when it was *do-or-die* , she took supper out of the disappointing device and served it up. They just about needed a sledgehammer to break it into bite-sized pieces. Luckily, they'd all had quite a few Mickey's, so no one except the cook noticed that the meal was a dismal failure.

That night Bob slept in his van, and Dick took the red iron guest bed in the basement.

* * *

After oatmeal the next morning, Dick and Bob went up behind the house to do a little scouting for moose sign before heading back to Anchorage. Poor guys. They both had city jobs to report to on Monday.

Dick and Bob went out to scout for moose.

Tim escorted them out, in case they had any trouble in the lake section, and Kate and the youngsters waved and watched the two rigs bump away.

When Tim returned home a half hour later, Kate was out tending her greens and the children were in the alder patch.

"Well, that was fun," Kate said when Tim came to stand beside her, "except for the supper. I thought that radar thing was supposed to cook food as fast as lightning."

"I thought so too," her mate replied. "But the guys didn't mind. They both asked me to thank you for a great time."

"But I wanted to dazzle them with my cooking. We have guests so seldom."

Tim looked at his free-spirited but slightly less-than-domestic young bride. "I think infrequent visits are great, as long as everyone leaves happy."

"Do you mean to say, rare visitors are fine, as long as they leave here well-done?"

He smiled at that. "Yup. That's just what I meant to say."

Kate reasoned, "I guess they came here for a wilderness experience, not the Ritz."

Exactly," her husband agreed. "And speaking of a wilderness experience, don't you think you're a little overdressed for gardening?" He gave her a sidelong glance.

"You wish," Kate grinned.

* * *

Then, all too soon, it was back to the city for another depressing winter.

* * *

Boom!

That spring, the price of oil crashed, and people began pouring out of Alaska like Dust Bowl refugees.

Tim and Kate grabbed the kids and clung to the frigid walls of their condo as if riding in a stateroom on the Titanic. Then, when they finally hit bottom, they paid the bank to take back their sunken city home.

Broke—and with their credit totally ruined—they were trapped in a financial tsunami that had been generated by world economies far beyond their control. Bad luck.

Go Toilet on the Mountain!

June 28—Dear Mamasan,

I am pleased to announce that the first toilet has been flushed on our mountain top! The auspicious event was followed immediately by a flood in the basement (which turned out to be the washer overflowing, and not the toilet, thankfully).

This means there will be no more trips to the laundromat, or to the privy, ever!

IT HAD TAKEN Tim nearly a year and a half to get Kate's throne plumbed in.

After a decade of waiting patiently, the two romantics quickly framed-in a fully-operational bathroom around the new crown jewel. When they were done, their new "Shrine of Running Water" held a tub that was big enough for the whole family to bathe in at once, a turquoise and translucent round shower, an old barber's sink (still sporting its original hoses and faucets), and a four-foot-tall laundry chute that dumped their soiled garments straight down onto the washer in the basement.

Kate had been storing twenty boxes of one-inch-square glass tiles down in Honeymoon Cottage since sometime in the seventies.

Now she hauled out the cases, one by one, carried them to the house, and began tiling. She worked right through several long, light-filled summer nights, while the children slept.

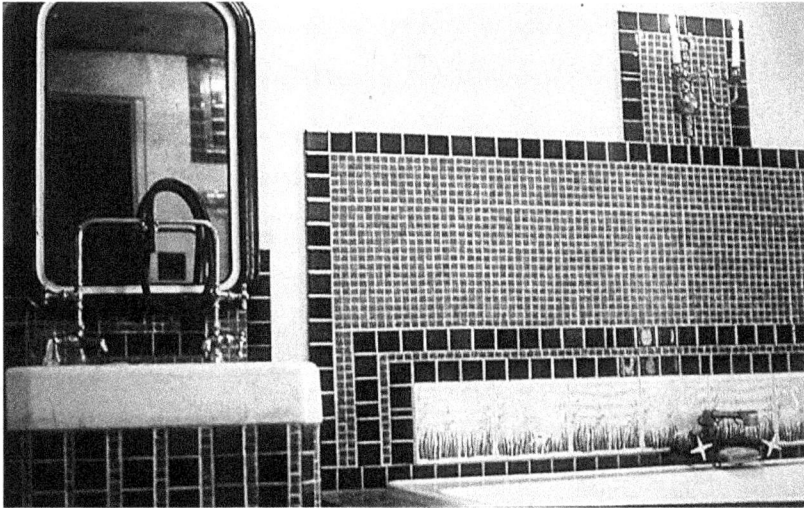

When Kate's Art Deco masterpiece was finished, the effect was stunning. Opening the bathroom door was like opening up a treasure box and the unexpected blast of shimmering turquoise just about blew a girl's socks off.

* * *

Not long after the "Shrine" was completed, Attie and Brew came up with a new game.

"Mommy, you don't have to check on us. We're fine. Okay?" As usual, Attie was the spokesperson.

Kate looked up. Two little faces were peeking around the corner. She watched as the impish smiles melted back into the hall.

Curious, she decided to see what her two little darlings were up to. She followed their secretive rustlings until she came to the bathroom door, which they had carefully closed.

When Kate opened the door, she found them perched on stools they'd dragged in. They were peering down into the tiled laundry chute with their little bottoms thrust out to keep them from falling as they leaned in over the open chute.

The bathroom shelves were half-empty and Brew looked poised to drop another bomb down onto the washer below. Kate was looking at a perfect Norman Rockwell composition.

Attie, who really had no idea what had

gone wrong with her plan, asked innocently, "Why did you check on us?"

Inside, Kate was laughing, but she immediately ordered a cease-fire.

* * *

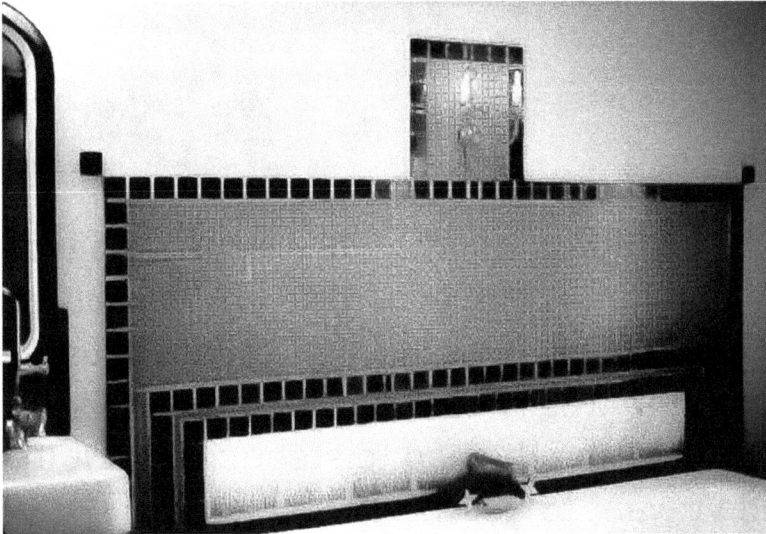

Whenever a rare guest did actually make it up to visit, and he or she asked to use the outhouse, Kate couldn't wait to say, "Sure. Go ahead." Then she would nonchalantly add, ". . . or you can use our Italian cut glass bathroom down the hall, if you'd rather."

It just killed her to be able to say that.

* * *

Only one thing bridled Brew's abandon that summer. The poor little boy was allergic to the plant that locals called "Pushki." Brewster was a towhead and, like his fair-haired mama, he had to steer clear of it if he didn't want to get a rash.

One day he came running home crying. He was all red and bumpy, so Kate put him in the bath to cool his burning skin. Both his mother and his older sister tried to teach him what to look for and how to avoid touching the plant, but Brew seemed unable to miss the stuff. He just couldn't resist charging pell-mell through the open field. So, Brew spent a lot of time soaking in the giant tub and playing with his washcloth porpoise.

July 12—Dear Tutu,
News from the hill:
Everything seems pretty quiet
around here, but we've only been home for
a couple of weeks. The biggest news so far,
is Brew's horrible Pushki (Alaskan cow
parsnip) rash. It's a huge bush with leaves
the size of a catcher's mitt. You'd think
he could see it coming, but he just crashes
right into it. So, he's in the tub a good
part of the time. Otherwise, it's all pretty
easy livin' here on the Last Frontier.
Love, Kate and the kids.

* * *

"Who wants to go for a ride in the wheel barrow?"

"I do!"

"I do, too!"

"Climb in. You can both fit in here."

Kate was finished gardening for the day. She took them for a ride around and between all the flower circles. "What are you two planning on doing this afternoon?"

"We're gonna have tea in our teahouse," Attie shared the news as if it was a secret.

"You have a teahouse?"

"Uh-huh. It's a *magic* teahouse."

"It's over there," Attie told her, pointing toward the alder patch.

With no snakes in Alaska, a magic spot in the alder sounded safe and fun. "Well, that's lovely."

"And we have a waterfall too," Attie said.

"A waterfall? Oh boy!"

"We slide over it," Attie said. "Watch!"

Kate watched delighted, as both children climbed up on top of a berm, slid down the long grass, and landed in a soft depression below. It was exactly the kind of play she and Tim had been envisioning for them.

July, 18—Dear Grandma Tutu,

No wonder people love Alaska in the summer. It's beautiful! We have long hours of sunlight now. True dark is four hours at most, with divine dawn and dusk pastels for an hour or two on each end. Getting the kids into bed by midnight is the hardest part of my day.

Love to you.

* * *

The weather that particular summer was mostly pleasant, so Attie and Brew spent many days exploring near the house.

Brew followed his big sister everywhere and Attie, who was three years older and knew a lot more than he did, sweetly showed Brew what she could.

On reassignment to Pump Station #4, and once again working three-weeks-on / one-week-off Tim finally had a chance to build the attached woodshed that had been part of Kate's original design for the house. It would also serve as an Arctic entry and a snow-machine drive-through port. Kate was hoping this would make winters there much easier. Maybe one day they would try a whole winter again . . . maybe when the children were grown.

With the woodshed done, Tim headed back to work, leaving Kate and the kids alone on the mountain for the next twenty-one days.

"Just split what you need for now, and when I get back, we'll rent a log-splitter and tackle the whole woodpile," he told her. "It'll sure look good when it's all split and stacked in this new woodshed, won't it?"

"It sure will, babe," Kate said, as she envisioned all the effort still required to achieve that glorious sight. "And remember, Ace and Cal will be here then."

"Good. Maybe they'll feel like splitting a few cords."

"We can make a party of it," Kate said, perking up at the thought.

Her big brother, Ace, and nephew Cal had been talking about coming up ever since nephew Cork had dazzled them with his stories about building the place, and they had both finally cleared their schedules long enough to actually make the trip. Hopefully, they wouldn't be the kind of guests who expected a night at the Ritz.

More Helpers

THREE WEEKS LATER, when Tim was back from Prudhoe Bay, the Peters family went to Soldotna to pick up Kate's oldest brother Ace, and good-old Cork's twin brother, Cal.

"Glad you came," Tim said, shaking his gigantic brother-in-law's hand, "especially if you feel like splitting some firewood while you're here." He'd presented the idea like a joke, but Kate knew he was serious.

"Sure! Lead the way!" Ace said.

"Great. Actually, we'll be stopping to rent a log-splitter in Footprint. If it works, that should make the job easy."

They grabbed the two Cuttings' satchels and headed for the M-37, with Tim driving and Ace up front beside him. Kate and Cal rode in the truck bed, backs against the cab, pinning the delighted children with their legs to keep them securely seated.

In Footprint they rented one of the dandy-looking splitter gadgets, threw it on the back of the trailer, and towed it home. When the trailer's leaf spring busted loose after bumping through one of the last holes in their long, rough driveway, it was determined that Ace, a welding hobbiest, could fix it when they got home. A couple of dips and bumps later, they were parking in front of Tim's shop.

Tim and Ace unloaded the log-splitter, and then all four teamed up to tip the trailer onto its side. Ace started welding on the broken leaf spring before he'd even gone inside the house, already doing what he loved.

"Welcome to Victory Garden," Kate said as she and Cal walked to the edge of the garden to admire the waves of fireweed billowing out below.

"Your view is petty Zen," Cal observed.

"Yes, isn't it?" Kate thought she knew just how her nephew was feeling and figured he was already soaking up some magic from the place.

They carried the groceries inside, and then went back out to assist Tim and Ace in uprighting the newly-repaired trailer.

Ace and Cal were two more "rare but well-done" visitors.

When the muddy tires landed with a bounce, Ace questioned the sunroof cutouts on both fenders. Kate told him the story of the good Samaritan with the portable welder.

"It was lucky he happened by when he did or I never would have gotten that load home. Gosh. That was ten years ago," Kate mused aloud; "ten years, and a thousand labors."

"Speaking of labor, what say we have some lunch and then try this baby out? We've never used one before, but it looks like it should work." Tim patted the log-splitter.

"Sounds good." Ace was smiling. The welding had revitalized him.

"Is that the privy?" Cal asked. He was pointing to Honeymoon Cottage.

"No, that's where you'll be sleeping. Cork slept there, too. The littler building with the moose antler over the door is the privy."

"Well, all right. I'm heading there now," Cal announced.

"You go ahead," his aunt said. "Or you could use the flush inside."

Cal was skeptical. "Cork said you guys just had an outhouse."

"Ha! Those were the old days. Let me show you around the place," Kate said with her usual dramatic flair.

They toured the upstairs, including the Shrine of Running Water—which Cal said he would be using immediately—and finished up in the basement.

After the grand tour, everyone wolfed down tuna sandwiches and well water. Then Attie and Brew headed off to meet Benny and Bobby at the tree house while the four adults went outside to tackle the splitting of what remained of their two hundred peeled logs.

Approaching the mechanical splitting device, Kate was envisioning Santa Claus possibly dropping one of the green genies down their chimney next Christmas. "How does it work?" she asked.

"You just lay the log in this cradle, and pull the lever . . . Presto!" Tim demonstrated.

He and Ace then took up positions on either side of the machine and began splitting logs.

"This isn't so bad." Tim was the first to say it.

"Piece of cake," Ace agreed.

After a few rounds, Cal spoke up. "You guys must have the easy job," the junior member of the crew panted.

"Is it time to trade yet?" Kate asked. "We should probably rotate." Cal and Kate had been carrying log sections over from the pile to the splitter, and then carrying the split wood into the woodshed and stacking it against the far wall, so they were both ready for a rest.

With some reluctance Tim and Ace relinquished their choice positions, and Cal took over the lever. He pulled, and the contraption made a perfect split. The log was now five sticks. He split three or four more sections.

"Okay, let me try it." Kate said, moving into position. "I put wood in; I pull lever; I watch men carry away and stack wood . . . I like it!"

After that, they rotated positions every five loads. That way no one got exhausted, and no one felt put-upon; and by the end of that first day they had about half the pile split and stacked. It was nine at night: time for corned beef hash.

"Let's call it a day," Tim suggested. "I'd say we've done an honest day's work."

"Whew!" Cal smiled. His teeth were the only part of him that gleamed in the fading light. Every other part of him was brown with sweaty dust. "Attie and Brew are two lucky kids to be growing up here." He looked around. "Where are they, anyway?"

"They're down at the tree house. They spend most of their time down there with Bobby and Benny. They're twins like you and Cork. They live on the other side of those woods. The four of them built a dandy tree house down there a while back, and that's been their main activity since."

Kate went outside and rang the dinner bell, signaling Attie and Brew to come home. The youngsters showed up about ten minutes later, looking filthy and happy.

"We'll have to take a number for the bathtub tonight," Kate said.

Ace and Cal stayed on the mountain for two nights, happily working shoulder to shoulder with the homesteaders. Between the four of them they got the whole pile of wood split and stacked.

* * *

When it was time for the travelers to catch their plane, Tim elected to drive them back to Soldotna while Kate and the kids stayed on the mountain to hold down the fort.

It was nice to see her relatives smiling as they climbed into the truck. Rare visitors or not, Kate's new aim was to have all departing guests head home feeling *well-worked and well-done*.

"Good-bye. Keep in touch!" Kate called out as they rolled away.

"We will! Thanks again for a *great* time!"

"Thank you for coming to visit, and thank you for all your help!"

Kate wondered again whether the reason they had so few visitors was because they tended to put their guests to work the minute they arrived. That was probably it.

Tim dropped off the log-splitter in Footprint and then drove Ace and Cal straight to the airport in Soldotna. He saw them off and was back by dark. Mission completed.

🌀 "The Voortrekker" 🌀

—Rudyard Kipling

THE GULL SHALL whistle in his wake,
the blind wave break, in fire.
He shall fulfil God's utmost will,
unknowing his desire.
And he shall see old planets change
and alien stars arise,
And give the gale his sea-worn sail
in shadow of new skies,

Strong lust of gear shall drive him forth
and hunger arm his hand,
To win his food from the desert rude,
his pittance from the sand.

His neighbours' smoke shall vex his eyes,
their voices break his rest.
He shall go forth till south is north
sullen and dispossessed.
He shall desire loneliness
and his desire shall bring,
hard on his heels a thousand wheels,
a People and a King.

He shall come back on his own track,
and by his scarce-cooled camp
There shall he meet the roaring street,
the derrick and the stamp:
There he shall blaze a nation's ways
with hatchet and with brand,
Till on his last-won wilderness
an Empire's outposts stand!

— 4 —

His Neighbours' Smoke Shall Vex . . .

Smoke Signals

IT WAS ANOTHER summer escape after a long winter's lodging in Anchorage.

Tim slowed the Gremlin at the bridge as its occupants stared out the car windows at the now vacant spot. Snyder's house was gone! Nothing remained but some garbage lying around. It was a pretty good bet that no one was living there now. Tim drove the family car through the former homesite, which had been a *dump* and was now a *ruin*.

"Where did their house go? Do you think whoever did this might have vandalized our place?" Kate asked Tim. He had to be thinking the same thing.

"We haven't given anyone a reason to be mad at us. Besides, I doubt if anyone even *saw* our place this spring," Tim said realistically.

"You're probably right. No one ever goes up past our place, except an occasional skier or hunter."

"And an occasional bear. If you want to worry about something, you can worry about bears," Tim suggested.

Kate looked around as they continued up the road, but she reported no bears or bear scat. When they got home, they found

Victory Garden undiscovered and unscathed. Good.

Tim would be off for a whole week, so he made it his first order of business to find out whatever he could about the mystery disappearance of Frampton Snyder's house. He went down the road to Bill O'Leary's to get the scoop, but Bill said nobody knew who'd taken Frampton's shack.

This made two suspicious acts on the mountain. There was the Goodmans' barn fire—which people now said had been arson—and Fram's house, which was simply missing. Puzzled, Tim went home to tell Kate what he'd discovered.

With Frampton gone, Kate secretly hoped the worst was over. She just wanted their neighborhood to be peaceful from this point on.

"Plus," Tim added, "Fram is still hanging around. Bill says Jared saw him on the road just yesterday."

"Oh great," Kate muttered.

* * *

June 27—Dear Double-Tutu,

We're back on the farm, safe and sound—sort of.

News of the neighborhood: Frampton is totally gone. This spring someone took his house! Weird, huh? The church members in Footprint have fixed the family up with a place in town, and Ruth has started a day-care center, so I guess she and her boys will be okay.

We don't know what Fram plans to do, now that his house is gone.

Other than that unlikely disappearance, the summer was starting off pretty well, with John and Melanie and the twins (now nearly eight) showing up just a few days after the Peters family returned. Attie and Brew didn't waste a minute getting together with Benny and Bobby down at the tree house.

But it wasn't long before the old animosities on Round Top Road billowed out again.

* * *

Jillian, who had been lobbying hard for a nice, smooth gravel road, ever since she'd first set foot on the mountain, had been to every meeting and begged every law maker on the Kenai Peninsula to allocate funding for the project. She'd also called upon everyone on Round Top Road to write letters asking for the same thing. As far as Jillian was concerned, this road was gonna get built, whether it *wanted* to be—or *not*. She wasn't asking for much—just a graveled road to her front door.

Jill's strong-arming might eventually win her that gravel, but it wasn't winning her any friends. Kate felt like she was being steam-rolled into pushing for a program that she wasn't sure she even wanted.

One day Jillian Radley asked both Melanie and Kate to write letters to the Borough, requesting (again) public funds. Kate listened halfheartedly and finally agreed to write, hoping that this would get Jillian to change the subject.

"I wish she'd just relax and enjoy the mountain the way it is," Kate said, when she and Melanie Read talked later.

"A gravel road means more people, and more people will mean more problems. I doubt a little gravel will be the panacea Jillian is expecting."

Melanie seemed to understand just how Kate felt, and she said she agreed.

Meanwhile, Tim and John Read, who both appreciated self-reliance and the independence it provided, had hit it off well right from the start. One sunny Saturday morning Tim brought up the subject of repairing the bridge. "With all this new traffic we may need to replace the bridge soon. It's looking bad. One of these days someone's gonna fall through."

"I can help," John said. He was strong as a bull.

An hour later, John and Tim were organized and outfitted for the task, and the two pioneers took their families down the road to address the task of repairing the bridge. Four willing adults offloaded the new timbers, while four eager youngsters rummaged for treasures.

"Keep away from the Snyders' old place," Kate instructed. "Stay on the far side of the bridge."

The foursome broke into self-appointed teams, with Kate and Melanie carrying new wood in and old wood out, and Tim and John replacing the worn planks. An hour into the operation, Carl Radley came through on his way to Footprint. He stopped with his front tires on one of the brand-new spans.

"What are you all up to?" he called out through the truck window.

"We're bracing up the bridge," Tim said. "Feel like giving us a hand?"

"I haven't got time right now. I'm on my way to town," Carl said. "Besides, why bother to fix it? We know the Borough's gonna gravel this road soon. And when that happens, they'll be putting in a culvert."

"A culvert?" Kate was surprised. "A culvert isn't nearly as picturesque as a bridge. Could they maybe just build a new bridge, instead?"

"No," Carl shook his head. "The proposal we submitted replaces this bridge with a pipe. It's a lot cheaper."

John turned to Tim. "Well, shall we continue?"

Tim shrugged. "It wouldn't hurt to shore it up a little while we're here," he said. "It might be a long time before the Borough does anything."

"Well, I gotta go." Carl said. Then he drove over the half-rotted bridge, leaving the fools to their mindless toil.

By evening, the Peterses and the Reads had put at least one more year of life into the old trestle, and they headed home feeling good about improving their access in the old-fashioned way.

Ford Flambé

THE PHONE HAD been ringing forever. Whoever it was, they weren't giving up. Rushing inside from the garden, Kate tossed an armload of fresh-cut kale onto the counter and raced to catch the phone before the caller hung up.

"Hello?"

An urgent voice shouted, "Hello, Kate? This is Bill O'Leary."

"Hi, Bill. What's up?"

"I just passed your truck down by the bridge, and it's on fire!"

"What?"

"Your red truck. I just saw it when I came in. It's on fire!" Bill shouted again.

"Good grief! I'm on my way. Thanks for letting me know."

"I'm headed back there now with my fire extinguisher," he said; and then he hung up.

Kate couldn't believe what Bill had just told her.

Their truck was on fire? Their 1974 extended-cab Ford pickup—which they'd just bought, and which she had only yesterday parked down at the bridge—was *on fire?*

Why would their truck be on fire?

She rounded up the kids and loaded them into the M-37, then she tore down to the bridge as fast as that old Power Wagon could maneuver.

When she got there, the truck was already dead—deep fried, in fact.

Attie burst into tears on the spot.

"Don't cry, little flower," her mother said, squatting down to hug her little girl.

"It's okay. We're all safe, and that's what counts."

"But I loved our red truck," she whined.

"I did too," her mommy told her, "for the whole week that we had it."

Meanwhile, Brew had picked up a stick and was poking it into a hole on the side of the road.

Kate stared at the carcass of what had been their newest and—until an hour ago— most comfortable family vehicle.

Bill walked over to the bewildered woman and her children. "It looks like it was a hot one. See that melted tire inside?"

Kate looked in the window and saw their spare tire melted right into the back seat. "How did our spare tire get inside?"

"Somebody put it in there, and then set fire to it," Bill said.

"Somebody deliberately set our truck on fire?"

"It looks that way," Bill said.

Did someone have a grudge against them, or was this just another act of random violence? Kate was baffled. This was the second suspicious fire up their road. Who was doing this? And *why?*

"Well, thanks for putting it out, Bill," Kate said.

"That's okay. It was already pretty much out when I got back. Well, I gotta get home. Pat will be worried. See you later."

Then Bill climbed into his shiny red pickup and drove away, leaving Kate and her children standing alone, perplexed in the middle of the forest.

When she got back to the house, Kate called the State Troopers. They said their man was out on a case right then, investigating some human remains discovered across Skilak Lake. But he'd be up as soon as possible, maybe even later that same day.

* * *

Tim, now assigned to work at ARCO headquarters in Anchorage five days a week, called home every night.

When he phoned that evening, Kate told him about the latest neighborhood arson.

"Someone set fire to our new truck?"

"That's what I said."

"The Ford is gone?"

"It was a big ol' Ford Flambé for a while, I guess."

Tim was silent for a beat. "Is everyone okay?"

"Yeah, we're all fine. I had it parked down by the bridge since it's been so rainy."

"Do we know who did it?"

"No. The trooper hasn't even been up yet. They found a body down by Skilak Lake and he's still checking that out."

"Will he be up tomorrow?"

"I don't know. Maybe."

"But you and the kids are safe?"

"Yeah, we're fine; but do you have time to say "hi" to Attie? This hit her pretty hard."

"Sure."

"She's right here."

Attie got on the phone and, for the first time all day, her face lit up as she talked to her daddy and he talked to her.

Kate finally took back the receiver.

". . . So, you're all fine?" Tim asked again.

"Yes. We're fine, just a little dumbfounded by the whole thing."

"I wish I was there, but I'll be home on Friday. 'Til then, you just keep the shotgun handy, okay?"

"I will. Good night, Timber."

"Good night, babe. Try not to worry. I'll be home in five days," he repeated.

* * *

Trooper Leeds got there to look at the truck on Wednesday, two days after the incident. Kate and the kids rendezvoused with him at the crime scene, and she told him everything she knew, which was basically nothing.

"How many people live up this way?" he asked.

"There are three couples and four kids up our road: The Reads, the Radleys, and us. And there are two single guys who own land, Jason Kanker and Butch Pratt; but they don't live up here yet. The O'Learys have the first place up the road on the right, and Jared Jones has the next place. Then the Curd brothers live all the way up at the slaughter house: that's Greg and Craig. And you passed the Tanner cabin as you came in. Also, there's a fellow named Cliff Deller who lives alone out on the flats. That's everybody I can think of."

The trooper was taking down all the names. "Have you had a quarrel with anyone recently?"

"No. We been trying to stay out of all the beefs."

"All the beefs?"

"Oh, you know, up here there's always something going on. If it's not the road, then it's the Fram thing."

"The Fram thing?" Leeds looked up, clearly waiting for more information.

"Frampton Snyder. He and his family were squatting here for years. They got evicted in 1982, but he's still around here a lot of the time."

It was hard for Kate to remain objective as she described all the junk Fram used to leave in the road, and all the manure everywhere. Then she told the trooper about Fram's lax animal-tending approach, and how a frustrated Bill O'Leary had shot Fram's pigs a few years back. Then Kate told Trooper Leeds about the first suspicious fire in the neighborhood, when Goodman's barn burned (also back in '82). And when she pointed to Fram's old place and told him the house had disappeared that spring, Leeds said he remembered hearing about the incident, but he had no more information.

The trooper wrote down everything she said in his spiral notebook. Then he looked up. "Okay. I'll do what I can, but I'm working on a suspicious death right now, so I may not be able to get to your case for a while. There are only two of us assigned to cover the western half of the Kenai Borough. And one of us is strictly on city duty."

"Does that mean you're the only lawman keeping the peace over a zillion square miles of rural Alaska?"

He grinned. "Yes, ma'am, it does. But half my territory is water, and most of the homes are right along the coast, so it's not really as bad as it sounds."

Kate shook her head. "Good grief! The Lone Ranger rides again. I guess my husband was right when he said we live in the Wild West."

"Yes, ma'am. Pretty much," Trooper Leeds said. "Anyway, good luck. Just call me through the headquarters switchboard, if you have any more trouble."

With a polite nod, the one and only law enforcement officer for the entire rural population of the western half of the Kenai Peninsula got into his mud-caked truck and drove away.

"Yeah, good luck, and keep your shotgun loaded," Kate mumbled to herself. She watched him disappear, and then she fished her little darlings out of the underbrush and drove them home. She would be on high alert until Tim got back on Friday.

$$* * *$$

That evening, Tim called to tell Kate that he'd taken care of everything. "You don't have to worry anymore. Everything's gonna be fine. I just bought us a new truck."

"You *did?"*

Well, that was a nice pick-me-up: a *brand-new truck*! Maybe this disaster would turn out to be a windfall, after all. The red extended cab had been tricky to drive, from the get-go. Whenever you needed to stop, you had to slam it into reverse. Out in the bush that worked fine, but at every intersection in town, the prospect of children flying around in the back seat had made Kate nervous for the entire week they'd owned it.

"That's great!" she said, now happy.

"Yeah," Tim went on. "I got a good deal on a Jeep. Just promise me you won't laugh when you see it."

"Not laugh?"

Kate's excitement folded like a poor hand of cards. It sounded like Tim was not talking about something new off the lot, but about a very-well-broken-in, funny-looking rig, instead.

"I'll drive it down there this weekend. It's a four-wheel drive. I paid six hundred for it. I think it's just what we need."

Kate assured him she'd be waiting with baited breath to see their newest family member. Then they talked about the trooper's visit; and about who could possibly have wanted to set fire to their nice truck; and about the children; and everything else that two lonely lovers talk about.

When there was nothing more to say, they reluctantly hung up.

* * *

Tim arrived in the replacement rig that Friday night. It was a Jeep, which was good. And, with the four-wheel drive he'd been able to get it right up to the front door, which was *great*. But Kate saw right away why he had cautioned her. The headlights were being held in place with old underpants.

Oh, why had she promised not to laugh?

"It looks good," she said, biting her lip to keep from breaking her vow. "What say we debrief those headlights one of these days soon?"

"Sure, okay," Tim acquiesced, although he didn't see the need.

JOURNAL ENTRY-JUNE 26

THINGS ARE HOT AROUND HERE (AND I DON'T MEAN THE WEATHER). SOMEONE SET FIRE TO OUR TRUCK THE OTHER MORNING, AND WE DON'T KNOW WHO, OR WHY.

I CAN SEE HOW A MAN MIGHT BE TEMPTED TO TAKE MATTERS INTO HIS OWN HANDS OUT HERE: WHEN YOU WANT THE LAW TO INTERVENE, IT CAN TAKE DAYS FOR A TROOPER TO SHOW UP.

* * *

Disagreements continued to smolder on the mountain that summer. Kate and Tim were fed up with the whole thing.

In late July, Tim took vacation time and they threw some stuff into a kit bag, and the family flew away to California for two weeks of bliss. They were hoping that when they came home in August, it would be to an all quiet Western Front.

O'Leary's Farmhouse Up in Flames!

WHEN THEY RETURNED from the Golden State, they found an even *bigger* stir going on. Someone had set fire to the O'Leary place! They heard about it when they stopped for milk and mail at the Sleeping Moose post office. Accusations were flying like shrapnel.

Ever on the alert, Tim decided to take a short detour to the O'Learys' before driving home on their own branch of the road.

The O'Learys' farmhouse following the fire.

"Wow! Do you know who did it?" Tim asked Bill when he saw the destruction.

"No. Not yet. But I have my suspicions."

"What did the trooper say?" Tim was asking.

"Oh, he doesn't know. A couple of gas cans were lying on the kitchen floor, so it was definitely arson."

"Bad luck. Do you think it was directed specifically at you?" Tim asked, surveying the damage.

"It's hard to figure, but the trooper thinks it's directed at us, yeah. He said your red truck was probably done by the same person—someone who mistook your truck for mine."

That was unfortunate; but it made sense. "What are you gonna do now?" Tim asked.

"Oh, we'll rebuild. Luckily, I'm insured," the Irishman said.

Bill had said something a minute earlier that was gnawing at Tim. "Well, we've gotta go," he suddenly announced.

He rounded up Kate and the kids and they headed back to the bridge and up their own hill.

He wanted to check his shop and count the gas cans.

"Well, whoever it was, they used *our* gas," Tim told Kate. He'd just come in from the shop. "There were two full cans when we left, and now they're missing."

"You mean the arsonist was up here?" This information was tough to digest.

"It looks that way."

"Does that mean we'll be suspects?"

"I doubt it. We weren't even in the state, and we have the ticket stubs to prove it. Besides, whoever it is, he burned our truck, too."

Kate was wading through the implications. "So that means they're not mad at *us* specifically, or it would have been *our* house they burned, not Bill's."

"Yup. It's O'Leary they're mad at, not us."

Kate breathed out. "Well, that's a relief . . . sort of."

Tim was still thinking. "It has to be someone who knew we were out of town. And that narrows it down to folks at the post office, or someone up our road.

Maybe we should hold up on the unpacking for now, just in case we need to get out of here in a hurry."

"Good plan," Kate agreed.

At Least We Can Save the Books

SHE COULDN'T SLEEP. "Timber?" Kate spoke softly, as they lay in bed that night.

"Hmmm?"

"I was thinking. What if whoever's doing this decides he wants to burn down *our* house?" This was a distinct possibility and they both knew it. "You know all our books?"

"Hmm." Tim wasn't moving his lips.

She went on. "They look perfect all lined up on their new shelves. You built us a beautiful library."

"Hmm."

"But if there *is* a fire, I'd hate to lose all the books."

Many of the volumes elicited cherished memories of her father. She had inherited them when he died. She'd chosen his art books, his mountaineering books, his Esperanto books, and a huge dictionary which always reminded her of the studious man who had drawn little pictures on her arms with a ball point pen. Sometimes he would even let her stand on his feet to dance two bars of *Waltz with Me, Henry* before making a hasty retreat behind his sound-proof study door.

"I'd feel better knowing that the books will be out of harm's way this winter. Even though Thoreau says to simplify, I still love our books." Tim, a history buff with his own collection, silently agreed.

Early the next morning they decided that it was about time for the whole family to head north anyway, so they moved up their departure date and planned an exodus. As soon as Tim got home on Friday they would pack up, and head out for the school year.

In the meantime, after breakfast they would start emptying the bookshelves; and when Tim left for Anchorage on Sunday, he would have a truck full of heirloom volumes with him.

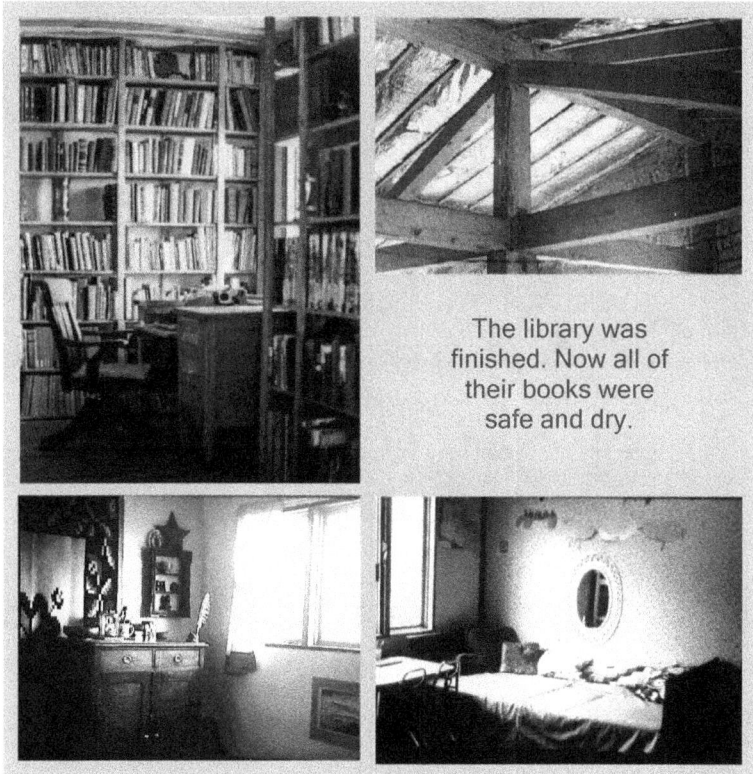

The library was finished. Now all of their books were safe and dry.

* * *

"Hi."

Kate was startled to look around and see the twins standing right behind her in the garden. They had walked up silently, with water cans in hand.

"Can we fill our water cans?"

"Sure. There's the hose."

The boys set down their cans and stuck the end of the hose into the hole in the top of the first can. When they were ready, Kate turned on the faucet.

"So, you guys are going back to Anchorage?" Benny asked.

"Uh-huh, pretty soon. Attie's school is starting."

"When will you be back?"

"We'll be back at Christmas, for sure, and maybe for a few days around Easter."

"Hmm." Benny was gazing at the loaded truck. "You sure got a lot o' books."

"Uh-huh. We're fools for these ol' things. We drag 'em around with us everywhere we go." She patted one of the volumes affectionately.

Suddenly Bobby spoke up. "Mrs. Peters, have you seen a little blue airplane around anyplace? I think I left it here somewhere, and I'd hate to not have it again 'til Christmas."

"I don't think I've seen it, but you're welcome to go in and look."

Both boys said, "Thank you," and went inside the house.

Kate left the can and went over to level out one book that was sticking up higher than the others. It was her father's big dictionary: six inches thick and with the fingerprints of her dad on most of the pages. She loved the thing. When she was satisfied with its placement, she went back to tending the hose and water cans.

After a minute the twins came back. "We can't find it." Bobby said, looking sad. "Can you help us look?"

Kate considered his request. These books were entirely vulnerable, lying there in the back of the pickup. Many a time an unexpected storm had caused damage to an unprotected load. She looked up at the sky. It was clear blue. No threat of rain.

"Okay, sure, Bobby. I can look with you. I think I know where it might be." She pushed the end of the hose deep-down inside the second can so it would slowly fill while they searched for the toy. "Let's go see if it's in Attie and Brew's room."

The three went in to the house.

"Is this it?" Kate had glimpsed a tip of blue wing peeking out from under Brew's snow boots. She leaned into the closet, grabbed up the toy, and handed it to Bobby. "There."

"Thanks Mrs. Peters," he said, visibly relieved to have the plane back in his hands.

"Sure. I'm just glad we found it." Kate answered, glancing out the side window to check on the water can operation. What she saw there went against all odds.

"*Oh, no!*" Kate shrieked as she raced for the door.

Never in a million years could she have predicted such a fluke. She dashed down the steps and ran to grab the head of a hose that was standing erect like a king cobra, spewing its venom twenty feet across the yard. Incomprehensibly, its lethal stream was aimed directly toward the back of the pickup truck, and the books were taking a bath.

She grabbed the revolting reptile by its rubbery neck and cut off its life source. At first the monster recoiled and then it died.

Kate rushed to the dozens of victims that now lay drowning in the back of the truck. They were all soaked.

"What *unbelievably* bad luck," Kate muttered as she surveyed the carnage. She offered comforting strokes to the volumes with puddles on their covers and murmured, "Oh, you poor old books!"

There really was nothing more to say. Kate struggled to assimilate this lesson. She would have to try to think of these books as *things,* rather than as *beloved* possessions.

"A person needs to be able to let go of things," she told herself silently.

It would be hard not to be mad at little Bobby, but this had been an accident; she knew that. She watched the twins struggle to carry the heavy cans full of water down the hill and tried to calm her ire. Their precious books had been damaged.

So what?

Kate went back and sat in the great room to recuperate from the shock. She let her eyes travel up along the golden beam-work that reached out to cradle the ceiling. Dark dribbles had stained some of them. A river of memories flooded her heart. It had taken a lot of work to cut, drag, and raise those pieces overhead. But even *they* were just "things," really.

"No!" Kate revolted from her defeatist thoughts. No! they were *not* just things. They were parts of a house that she and Tim had built with blisters, and lots of stubborn determination. This home was the consummation of endless effort, and she would not let their dream slip away!

Even as she vowed to persevere, a sobering fact settled in the back of her mind. One day, they might actually have to let go of everything up here . . .

Later that afternoon, when Tim drove away with the soggy tomes, Kate waved goodbye to him, went inside to weep for a moment, and then she begin packing for their next long winter in the city.

September 13—Dear Tutu,

We just got back to Anchorage and took out fire insurance on Victory Garden. We had to pay a king's ransom, of course, since it's vacant most of the time, and especially now, with all the arsons. But fear not. We're safely sequestered for the coming winter.

Attie's in first grade and reading like a scholar. It'll be just Brew and me holding down the fort most of the time. Maybe we can have some good philosophical discussions while studying the hoarfrost outside.

Home burns, troopers probe series of mysterious fires

* * *

Autumn actually scurried by, since Tim was still working at ARCO headquarters in Anchorage and he could be home every night, like a normal breadwinner.

Attie was flourishing in her new class, which was good. Kate spent most days watching Brew climb and fall and learn, which seemed to be the only things one could do in a frozen, icy city.

On nice afternoons she and Brew went outside,but Anchorage—not known for its nice weather—kept them inside, feeling cramped and isolated most of the time. Kate missed the good times she'd had in Fairbanks, with dancing and friends, and plenty of activities within walking distance.

Making the most of a rare, nice day in the coastal city.

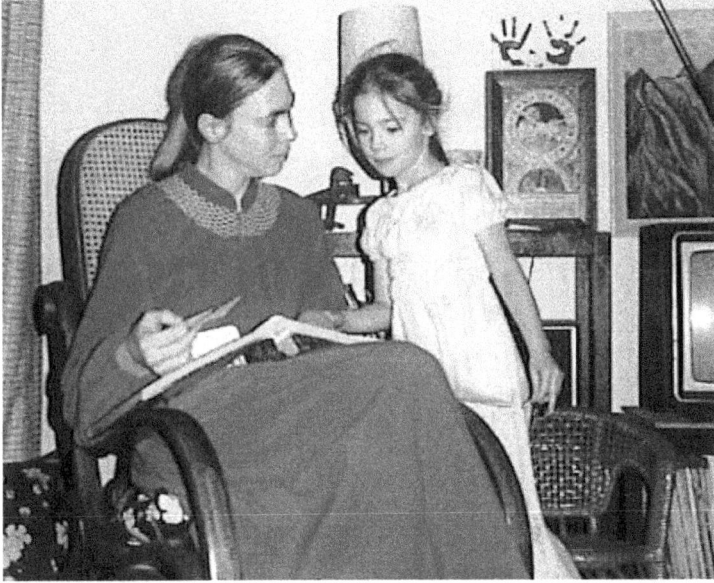

Then, it was Christmastime and Tim would be off for two whole weeks.

They headed south as soon as Attie's school dismissed for the holidays.

Feud

"IF *THEY'RE* COMING, then we're *not!*"Jillian Radley's refusal had been immediate and emphatic when Kate called to invite the Radleys to a Christmas party at Victory Garden.

"If you're not *with* us—then you're *against* us," Jillian added, further clarifying her feelings. Then she hung up.

"Well, I guess this means they're not coming," Kate told Tim, hanging up as well.

He shrugged. "That's okay. Who wants hard feelings at a party? Don't forget how the Curds' shindig ended."

Carl and Jillian's road campaign had pretty much polarized the neighborhood and —by default—people were choosing up sides.

Kate and Jillian clearly didn't share identical passions. Their neighbor (secretly referred to as **"the Malamute Madam"** by some), was so doggedly fixed on upgrading the road that it was the only thing she talked about. Kate sometimes ducked behind the counter when she saw the woman approaching.

But it could make things difficult, and maybe even dangerous to be counted as enemies of the Radleys, since the Peterses' driveway went right past Carl and Jillian's turnoff. And it also threaded between the two parcels owned by Butch and Jason at the top of Goodman's upper field. If someone wanted to stop them from coming through, they could do it right there, at the only high pass through the Moose Flat marsh.

So far, it had behooved Tim and Kate to be nice about the whole thing, but that was getting harder and harder to do. Now, Jillian's line-in-the-sand felt like the last straw.

"Darn it," Kate growled. "Can't we all just get along and go back to those good old days of peace and nudity for all? Call me Switzerland, but I don't want to be involved in *any* part of it!"

Tim and Kate held mixed feelings about graveling the road, state money or no. After all, the Goodmans had gotten along just fine without a road—sort of. And besides, if access got any easier, it would mean more strangers coming up to ski and hunt, and maybe to pillage and plunder. At any rate, a graveled road surely wasn't worth going to war over.

By this time, all the Round Top residents' letters and Jillian Radley's persistent presence at meetings had earned the once-remote enclave a reputation as "that bunch of troublemakers who want their own private road at public expense."

That image didn't seem to worry Jillian, and she pressed on with verve; but a few of the others were not comfortable being viewed as problems by residents of the county.

Despite some borough dollars which had eventually trickled down their way, the Peterses found that getting home on the range hadn't gotten any easier. In fact, now it felt worse.

It seems Kate's invitation to the holiday bash had coincided with some bad blood that was brewing between former best friends, the Radleys and the O'Learys.

Here was Kate's take on the situation. Jillian, who had procured the funds pretty much through her concerted efforts alone, felt that she had earned the right to have the gravel run her way. Kate could see that side of the argument.

Bill O'Leary's point, however, made better community-development logic. With only a little more work, the main fork could be connected to a second dead-end road, which would provide a shortcut loop to and from the highway. He argued that the left fork would be more costly, and less likely to receive additional borough funding to complete the project. Of course, by going straight at the bridge, the gravel would, in essence, run right past *O'Leary's* instead of up to the Radleys' place.

This made Jillian *furious!*

From that point on, their disagreement had pretty much become a feud, and Jillian Radley had Bill O'Leary in her crosshairs.

Now Tim had a suggestion. "We don't have to have a Christmas party this year."

Kate agreed, and they cancelled all plans for a party.

Instead, they cut d o w n a nice-looking tree a n d ornamented i t with coffee can rims and holiday cards they'd received from loved ones.

As soon as their private festivities were over, the family packed up and headed back to Anchorage without any fanfare at all.

You Can't Beat the Water

SIX MONTHS LATER, the Peters Family was on their way south, once again.

June 14—Dear Mamasan,

We're on our way to the mountain at this very moment! Both kids are sound asleep in the back seat. (We left at 5:00 this morning.) We're hoping the road has hardened up by now, but we'll just have to wait and see when we get there.

When they arrived at the bridge, the road looked so dry that Tim thought they could probably drive all the way up to the front door. That would make a nice start to the extended stay.

As they crossed Neil Goodman's upper field, they saw that one of the bachelors was building a little house for himself right at the top of the hill. Jason Kanker, the bush pilot and guide, was moving in!

"His house looks pretty close to the road, don't you think?" Kate asked Tim.

"Yeah, but we can still get by."

Seeing that Jason was pretty far along with his building project, and comfortable with the fact that their right-of-way was legally deeded, Tim stopped to say hello. He reminded the neighbor about the easement.

Jason said that he understood, and it wouldn't be a problem. After a short and pleasant exchange, Tim nodded and pulled on past Kanker's place.

Kate was thinking about the time she'd hunched behind the sled in a whiteout, waiting for Tim to come back to rescue her and the groceries. She'd thought she might die in the ice right there that night. And now a fellow was fixing to live on *that exact spot*. Wow, the place was sure changing.

A half-mile later, they were home.

After piling out and stretching, Attie and Brew darted away to begin discovering forgotten delights.

"Let's see if the teahouse is still there."

"Yeah. Let's go see the teahouse," Brew cried happily.

"I'll lead the way," Attie said.

"I know the way," Brew opposed. "Let me go first!"

"No! I'm bigger!"

Brew couldn't argue with that, so he looked around the yard for different inspiration. His eye lighted on one of the toy wooden swords they'd left lying against the basement wall.

"I don't want to go see the dumb ol' teahouse," he suddenly informed his sister. "I want to play with this!" He picked up the sword and began practicing his strokes with aplomb.

"That's *my* sword. Give it back!" Attie hollered, grabbing for it.

"No! I had it first." Brew swung the sword at Attie's leg, which was within range; and when it walloped her, she cried out.

"Ow! Mommy, Brew hit me with a sword!"

Kate gave their father a sidelong glance. "Looks like there's already trouble in paradise," she said.

"Yes, but it's nothing we need to worry about," Tim said. "At least the neighborhood didn't go up in smoke while we were up north."

There had been no recent arson episodes on the mountain, and they'd seen no dead bodies strewn along the roadside as they were driving up. Both were good signs.

"Timber, what do you think will happen as more people come to settle up here?"

"Only time will tell," he said.

Kate nodded wisely. "I know: 'Does a bear shit in the woods?' I wish things were still the way they were when we first got here, when there was no one else around except the Goodmans."

"Me too," Tim agreed. He took hold of the Master Lock securing the basement door. "Well, are you ready?"

"Ready," his First Mate confirmed.

Tim removed the padlock and slid back the huge bolt. Then he pulled the latchstring and opened the door.

"It looks good inside," he said, stepping down into the basement. Kate followed him in. It was dark and chilly.

"What's this doing here?" Kate was looking down at her laundry basket. It lay twenty feet from the laundry area.

Meanwhile, Tim was curious about several pieces of lumber lying in a jumble in the old kitchen area. "I didn't leave all this lumber thrown around. Who moved everything? Someone's been in here," he said.

Kate thought about the recent arsons. "I hope everything's okay upstairs," she said as she started for the interior stairs.

"Wait a minute," Tim said, calling her back. "I think we had a flood here."

Tim was pointing to a perfectly horizontal mark running all the way around the metal sides of the furnace. It was about two feet above the floor. "Look at this water line on the furnace. It's on the basement walls, too."

"Oh no, a broken pipe!" The woman immediately felt guilty, since it had been she who had begged for indoor plumbing. "Oh, Timber, I'm sorry I insisted you put in running water."

"I don't think it was your water, Kate. I emptied all the pipes before we left. No, I think it came up out of the ground."

"It did?"

Relieved, Kate now wondered whether this would be be an ongoing problem for them.

A lot of stuff had been floating around. Now that they were focusing on it, they could see all sorts of flotsam where it didn't belong. It was lying everywhere: floating around at high tide, and snagged haphazardly as the water receded.

There were a few items, like a year's supply of powdered laundry detergent, that had been destroyed, but for the most part things had just moved around.

"Well, anyway, we've got some work ahead of us here. Let's go upstairs and let the kids in," Kate suggested.

"Oh yeah, the kids."

"Yes, Mountain Man, the kids. Let's go upstairs. I'm so glad to be home."

* * *

Tim stayed just long enough to see everyone settled in. He needed to head back to Anchorage that Sunday afternoon.

He was already in the car, and Kate was standing by his window, procrastinating. "You shouldn't have any trouble with the Jeep," he said. "I oiled 'er up for you."

"Thank you." Kate held his hand. "I wish you didn't have to go."

"You just have fun with Attie and Brew and try to stay out of any neighborhood squabbles."

"You've got that right. If we see anyone coming, we're gonna hide behind the sofa."

"Good. Okay, you and the kids have fun while I'm away. Maybe you can finish straightening up the basement." Tim adjusted his polka-dot welder's hat and started the engine.

"Okay, my love," Kate said. "You have fun at ARCO."

"Ha-ha. Yeah. Well, I guess I'd better go. I'll see you guys next weekend."

"We'll be right here, waiting for you."

Kate leaned in the window and kissed her mate good-bye. Then he engaged the gear and slowly pulled away.

Attie and Brew trotted down the road after him, waving and calling out until the family's little green car had disappeared into the woods.

They all found things to do for the rest of that day, and in the evening, they snuggled and talked about how much they missed their daddy. Then they all went to bed at ten o'clock. It was barely dusk.

* * *

"Drat! It's always something!" The next morning Kate spied a moose nibbling on one of her transplanted birches. She opened the door and waved her arms. "Move along, little doggie!"

The bull moose looked up as he continued chewing on his morsels.

This clear lack of concern reminded Kate of one of Tim's truisms: "You only own what you can protect."

The gardener would have to be more assertive. "You! Moose! Be gone!" She took a menacing step out the door toward the hulking animal.

The moose looked up and snorted. Then he stretched out his long legs and trotted away down the hill, with dewlap swinging from side to side like a bell clanging from his throat.

Kate watched the long-legged animal go, and envied the moose's ease of travel through Alaskan hummocks and underbrush.

"You are definitely meant for this terrain," she mused, "but my trees are never gonna grow if you don't stay out of my garden." She looked over at the pile of log slabs behind the greenhouse and began picturing a tall moose fence around her garden. Maybe she could start the project while Tim was away, and surprise him.

. . . Who was she kidding? She would never be able to build a fence without Tim. Kate sighed and wished she could do more on her own. There would *always* be a pile of jobs waiting for Tim when he got home, poor guy.

Pretty soon the children padded out into the great room, and Kate took up her duties as Mother.

"Good morning, you two. How would you like pancakes for breakfast?"

Weasel Mechanics

WHEN TIM ARRIVED home the following Friday, he started his first task immediately. "The Weasel's gone off kilter," he told Kate. "Can you come out and hold the light for me while I take a look at it?"

"Sure."

* * *

That "look" ended up taking all afternoon and early evening, with Tim hanging upside down through a trap door in the floor the whole time. This was the only way to access the engine, so Kate was shining the flashlight down into the hole with one hand and holding onto one of his back pockets with the other.

Tim came up for air. "There's no way to get at anything down there."

"Let's take a break. I'll cook a nice supper, and you can rest—right-side-up, for a while ."

"Good. I need a break." That evening during supper Tim said, "Back in the Army they used to say, 'A Weasel owner is a Weasel mechanic.' They sure had that right."

"Daddy, can we go for a ride in it tomorrow?" Attie spoke and Brew sat, spoon poised in midair, waiting for the answer.

"We'll see. We'll see."

They both pushed harder. *"Please?"*

"We'll see. I've gotta fix it first," their dad said.

After supper, the kids went out to play for a while and their mom and dad went back to work on—or more accurately—*in* the Weasel.

* * *

"My hand's asleep. I can't hold this flashlight one more minute," Kate finally said. "Let's take a break."

She'd been standing bent at a forty-five-degree angle, holding the light poised over the hole, for several hours now; and she thought she was about to crack open.

"Okay. But I want to get this thing running tonight."

"No problem. I'll go put the kids to bed, and be right back."

Kate hauled upwards on Tim's belt loops as he wormed his way out of the engine box, and when they walked out of the shop together, they stepped into the stunning daylight of an Alaskan mid-summer's night.

Kate could hear Attie and Brew playing out in their magic teahouse.

"Come on kids, bedtime."

"But it's still day," they both protested immediately.

"It's midnight: time for bed." Outmaneuvered, they surrendered and grumped into the house.

"Make sure you wash your face and hands and brush your teeth. Then get into your pajamas, and call me when you're ready for a story."

They complied, and Kate read them a story. Then she tucked each child in with a goodnight kiss and started out the door. Their mother stopped and turned. "Do *not* get out of those beds," she ordered.

The wool blankets she'd hung over the windows *almost* made the room dark enough to pretend it was night outside, but not quite, and their little bodies were already wriggling by the time she had the door closed.

"Go to sleep, you two," she said again. By the time Kate got back to the shop Tim had already lowered himself upside-down into the belly of the beast. She leapt in to assist, and they worked like that—he submerged, and she reeling him upwards—until five in the morning.

"Okay. The starter's hooked up. Can you get me out of this hole?"

"I'll try," Kate promised. "I'm not sure I can move." She clenched and unclenched each fist twice and then hauled up on his pants. Tim came out like a Caesarian breech.

When they were both standing upright outside of the Weasel, Kate suggested, "Let's get some sleep. If *I'm tired*, *you* must be *exhausted*."

"No argument here," Tim admitted.

Fifteen minutes later they both fell into bed, and they found themselves staring at an already-risen sun.

"I'll take care of that," Kate said. She grabbed at an old bedspread she had stored under the bed. When she snapped the cloth open, a little scrap of paper fluttered out and landed on the bed.

"What's this?" Kate scooped up the dust-covered missive, then smiled when she recognized the handwriting.

"Hey, Tim, it's our original five-year plan. Do you want to see how far down the list we've gotten?"

"Sure," he said. "Lay it on me."

She read the list aloud, and they verbally checked-off each deed together:

"Starter cabin?"

"Check."

"Basement?"

"Check."

"Henhouse?"

"Check."

"Greenhouse?"

"Check."

She went on. "Gas shed?"

"Check."

"Shop?"

"Check."

"Upstairs?"

"Check."

"Running water? ...*Check!*"

"Barn? . . . Nope."

"Corrals? Nope."

"Road?"

"Hmmm. Probably never . . ."

It was uplifting to see that they'd finished almost everything that they had expected to complete in the first year. And it had only taken a decade.

Kate continued reading all the way down to the end. It was going faster now.

"Moose fence?"

She paused. "I'd hoped we could start on that this weekend, but now I doubt that's gonna happen."

"Wood shed?"

"Check."

"And that's all," Kate said, nodding with satisfaction.

Tim stopped her. "Wait a minute. You forgot one," he said.

"I did? Where?"

"Right about there." He pointed to a spot three fourths of the way down the page.

"What did I miss?"

"Bury husband." Tim said, completely straight-faced.

The joke made Kate worry. "Oh Timber, am I working you too hard?"

"Nope," he said, "just right." He smiled. "But one day let's go over to the far ridge, to that spot where I said I wanted to be buried. I've been thinking we might build a guest cabin over there."

"Shall I put it on the list?"

"Sure, go ahead."

"Okay." Kate took the pencil from her bedside table and added "guest cabin" to the page.

"There."

Then she slipped the list away in the drawer, tacked the bedspread up over the window, and darkened the room to twilight.

"Now let's get some sleep."

"Okay. Good-night, babe," Tim murmured.

"Good-night, dear," Kate said, as she climbed into bed beside him. "Actually, I should say 'good-morning.'"

"Okay. Good-night." Tim said again. He was already half-way out.

* * *

The kids were up at eight. Since their mom and dad were being such big-old sleepyheads, they got their own cereal and went out to play.

When their parents finally rose, the family spent Saturday afternoon and all day Sunday logging trees and hauling firewood home behind the Weasel.

Tim and Kate worked on the wood, while the children climbed in and out and all over the Weasel. The rig was a portable playhouse, as well as the bush family's station wagon.

Luckily, the starter worked fine and the whole thing turned out to be a jolly outing.

The Kids liked to climb around on their portable playhouse.

Free to Grow

TIM HAD A whole week off just before the end of summer. The season had gone by fast, and now all the verdant shrubs were switching to golds and reds.

"Who wants to go pick blueberries?" he called out on his first morning back.

"We do! We do!" Attie and Brew both came running out of the alder, always ripe for an adventure with Daddy.

"Good." Tim said. "Hop in the back of the Jeep."

They howled with pleasure while Kate fussed.

"Do you think they'll be safe back there? There's no tailgate."

"They'll be fine. You need to let 'em grow, Katie girl."

The children were jumping up and down in the truck bed, thrilled with this new independence.

Reluctantly agreeing to let them sit in the back, their mother shouted out guidelines for them from her place in the cab. "You kids stay sitting down, and hold on!"

Her instructions dissipated into the bright blue sky, completely unenforceable from where she sat in the cab.

Unchecked, Attie and Brew crawled around and squiggled and had a great time in the back of the truck while their father drove at a crawl. The youngsters bobbed happily up and down as the family truck tipped and boi-oinged down the hill. They were out for a fun family holiday.

Kate had known more than one victim of a severe head trauma, and she was not at all sure this was a good idea, but she guessed if they were ever going to fall out of the back of a pickup, then a slow-moving truck in the middle of a soft field was probably the best place for such a valuable life lesson. Tim must know what he was doing. She held her breath.

"Yippee! Yippee!" Brew was shouting. "Yippee!" Attie echoed. "Yippee!" Then, Attie suddenly sounded frantic. "Stop, Daddy! *Stop!* Brew fell out!"

In an instant, Tim had pulled to a halt and Kate had opened her door and was jumping out; but Tim gently held her back. "He's okay, Mama. Let him toughen up a little."

Tim opened his door and craned his head around to look at his son. "Are you okay Brew?"

"I'm okay, Daddy."

"Good. Do you need any help getting back in?"

"No. I can do it. I'm a big boy."

Brew worked at it, and finally climbed up onto the bumper and crawled into the open backend, with a better understanding of truck-bed passenger decorum than driver's ed ever could have taught him.

Kate exhaled at last. "Good job, Papa!"

Once firmly seated, the family sashayed on down to the blueberry patch. Everything smelled rich and potent down in the bog; and they picked two coffee cans full of blueberries, all the while drinking in the heady elixir of forest around them.

The ride home had the same seating arrangement. Smarter now, no one fell out.

After supper, while the kids were outside climbing around on stuff, Tim asked Kate if she wanted to go blueberry picking again in the morning.

"Gee, I think we have enough blueberries for the time being. But it was fun."

"Well then, tomorrow maybe I'll go watch the kids slide down the zip line at their tree house."

"You do that. I'd sooner bake a pie than stand there and watch them risk life and limb at the top of a tree."

Tim's hopes lifted at the word. "You're gonna bake a pie?"

"No. That was just a figure of speech." Then she looked at her man. ". . . But I might try cookies."

"Cookies would be good."

Kate smiled. "We're glad you're home, Daddy. We miss you when you're away."

"I miss you guys, too."

"Well, tomorrow the kids can show you what they've been up to. They'll be excited. And I'll try baking cookies for you. And we'll have another perfect day."

Tim's tree house tour turned out to be a delightful excursion back into his own suburban Boston childhood. Then school beckoned, and it was time for the family to migrate again. Another seasonal swing of the pendulum.

* * *

JOURNAL ENTRY-
NOTES FROM THE CITY
HOW DO I RECORD THIS WINTER? TOTAL DARKNESS IN A HOME WITH NO YARD; AND CITY DRIVING ON ICE —WHICH IS OKAY—AS LONG AS YOU DON'T NEED TO STOP OR TURN.
ALL THE USUAL "URBAN ARCTIC WINTER" STUFF, I GUESS.
I AM DEPRESSED.
I NEED A JOB—OR AT LEAST A PROJECT.

The City in Winter

THE ANCHORAGE SIDEWALKS were littered with dog droppings, and thanks to the thawing and freezing of its seaside setting, the streets were usually sheer ice.

Kate always felt cold. She never could get warm when sitting in their trendy sunken living room. The modern architecture seemed flawed, sucking heated air out through the fireplace and replacing it with the refrigerated remnants of a futile fight between furnace and frigid subfloor. Plus, the place was always in shade.

By Christmastime, she and the kids were ready to break free from their sealed envelope of an urban-home.

As soon as Tim's vacation started, the Peters family high-tailed it down to Sleeping Moose. They were all more than ready for some snowy holiday fun.

When they got to Victory Garden, all was quiet, with not a neighbor in sight. Perfect!

It felt so peaceful—like the old days.

The matching sleds got a fine workout, and Santa came on time; and everything about their holiday was perfect, except that it was over *way* too soon.

* * *

January 3—Dear Mamasan,

We're just back from several dandy days on the mountain. No one was around, so we had a nice respite, with lots of sledding and hot baths and cocoa and crystallized sunrises. It was cold in the morning when we first woke, but then we got the fire going and the place warmed up. Fun, fun.

I love all the smells down there, like wood smoke and log oil. And our well-water tastes so pure, and the air is so fresh . . . but don't get me started.

It's weird having two houses: you never know where your spatula is, or whether there's extra toilet paper in the closet. Maybe someday we'll have a normal life, like other people—then again, maybe not.

That spring, Kate found work in a greenhouse keeping people's geranium baskets alive over the winter. Traditionally they were reclaimed on Memorial Day to hang from household eaves. Those brilliant colors instantly livened up the place after nine months of cold white nights. Kate decided that working there, spending the day surrounded by those masses of sheer beauty, was the *only* way to spend a winter in the city.

* * *

The first part of the next summer went smoothly on the mountain, even though tension between the O'Learys and the Radleys had grown palpable.

The twins came up to play every day, and Tim and Kate did what they could to steer clear of the feud over the road—which was definitely a damper, but not a deal-breaker.

They were still living in their perfect place, and the inconvenience was worth it, dammit!

—5—

An Unhealthy Number of Malcontents

Much Too Close to Home

BY MID-JULY a gauntlet had been thrown down and a duel between the two road adversaries seemed imminent. Victory Garden was on alert. One Saturday morning Kate saw two figures walking through the meadow. "Heads-up. We've got visitors," she warned. "I'm not sure who it is."

She squinted to see them better. "Wait, I think it's Charlie and Augusta Myers."

Tim, who was home for the weekend, studied the visitors for a moment, and then agreed with her assessment. "Let's get that coffee going," he said.

They watched the progress as the pair made their way up from the flat. It was the Myerses, all right. They were coming overland, following a burn scar left by that grassfire a few years back. A shortcut across the flat took miles off the trip, and could avoid untold problems if they were to run into Frampton.

"Welcome, friends!" Tim called out as they got close. "Care for some coffee? We've got some on."

"Don't mind if we do," Charlie said.

"It'll be ready soon," Kate said, smiling.

Tim told Charlie he wanted to show him the wood-heated machinery shop while they waited for the coffee, and Kate was excited to show Augusta their glass-tiled bathroom.

"We'll call you when the coffee's hot."

When Charlie and Tim got to the shop Tim pointed out where the two gas cans had been. "Whoever burned the O'Learys', they used my gas to do it," he said.

Charlie shook his head. "There've been too many fires around here lately, that's for sure. Say, did you ever find out who burned your truck?"

"No. It could've been anyone."

"Too bad." Charlie offered. Then he broached the news that they'd come to share. "Say, did you hear about Fram's boy?"

"Orvis?"

"No. Young Jimmy. He just got hisself arrested for molesting a bunch of little tykes down there in Footprint."

"Ruth's son, Jimmy?"

"Yes sir. You know she runs that day care center down there in Footprint. Well, now come to find out, her own little helper was helping *hisself* while she was away, if you know what I mean." Charlie Myers lowered his voice as he saw the women come out the door and head for the garden. "Yup, that boy came to no good. He's up to jail in Anchorage now."

Tim was shocked. "When did this happen?"

"I guess it's been going on right along, for the past year or two. It's a real shame."

. . . Meanwhile, out in the garden Augusta was telling Kate the same shocking news.

"*What?*" Kate gasped, incredulous. Then, when she realized how narrowly they had dodged a bullet, she decided that gut reactions were dependable after all. "If they'd settled on our doorstep the way Frampton first wanted to, that would have been *our* babies Jimmy was raping, and no one else's." She shuddered. Then both she and Augusta shook their heads.

A few minutes later, all four of them met up in the great room, where the discussion about Jimmy continued.

"That's really horrible! That's really *very* bad," Kate murmured into her coffee.

"But he's not the *only* rapist we've had up here," Augusta said, making this next tidbit sound mysterious.

"Really?" Kate didn't want to hear that there were more pedophiles around.

"Yes sir. That boy whose father rents Curds' slaughter house, he raped a girl last fall up near Kenai Lake," Augusta said.

"Is he back down here now?"

"Naw. You don't need to worry about him," Charlie said.

"Oh, he's in jail?" Kate pressed—because she *was* worried about him.

"Oh, they locked him up for a while, but he got out . . . last March, wasn't it, Auggie?"

Augusta nodded.

Charlie went on. "Then, less than a month after his release, he got hisself stabbed in a knife fight. Died right there, on the spot." Myers, who had come to the end of his story, sounded pleased with this satisfying finish.

Kate was aghast. "What *is* it with this place?"

"Well, what do you expect?" Augusta asked with knit brows. "It's the *strange* ones as lives at the end of a lonesome road like yours."

That was it! Kate suddenly realized that Augusta was right. *They had built their house at the very end of a difficult road, which itself headed away from the edge of civilization and went a few miles out from there. Mix in a human cluster with that element of isolation and hide them at the end of a mud road, and you'd find a high percentage of individuals who aren't afraid of the law, and prefer to handle things in a more rudimentary method than is acceptable within most societies.* She reasoned all of this silently to herself.

"The problem is," Charlie, who had taken back the floor, summarized, "there's no law up here. Troublemakers feel like they can do whatever they want."

Kate counted up the violent events that had occurred since they'd settled on the mountain. Calculating roughly, she thought maybe *a third* of their twenty nearest neighbors would use unlawful force to get what they wanted.

"Yep," Augusta was back to the news about Jimmy and Fram, "I never did trust Frampton, after we found him in our bed with those piglets."

"Yeah, he mighta taught little Jimmy some bad habits," Charlie added.

Kate volunteered a comment. "Well, I'm sure glad they didn't settle right here on our doorstep. That would have been our own personal tragedy."

"That's for sure," Augusta agreed. "Life is hard enough up here without the likes of Fram and his brood to bother with. He never was 'right,' you know. They say he got kicked in the head, way back."

"Or maybe it's 'cause he has a harelip," Charlie mused aloud.

Kate hoped Charlie was kidding.

The ghastly news all delivered, the old homesteader stood up and put on his hat. "Well, Auggie, it's time to go," he announced.

They said a first round of goodbyes at the front door and stepped out onto the stoop. After some second salutations, Charlie and Augusta descended the steps and started walking away through the meadow toward home. Kate and Tim stood in the open door, watching them go.

"Incidentally, Augusta," Kate suddenly called out, "You were right. It took *exactly* ten years to do what I thought we'd have done in one."

Augusta Myers turned and gave the younger settler a knowing nod.

Kate watched the old couple walk away down through the pasture land.

"I hope I don't look as discouraged now, as Augusta did that first time we met," she said.

"Don't you worry—you still look great, especially when you're wearing nothing but your boots."

Kate gave him a little hip check, and went back inside to process the disturbing facts she'd just learned.

JOURNAL ENTRY
FOR SUCH A TINY POPULATION,
WE DO SEEM TO HAVE A LION'S SHARE
OF FEUDING ARSONISTS AND RAPISTS UP HERE.
WHATEVER HAPPENED TO GOOD OLD
APPLE PIE, HONOR, AND THE AMERICAN WAY?

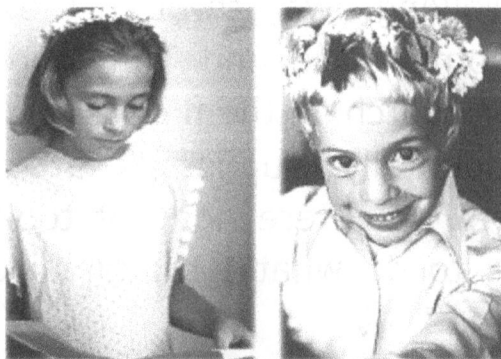

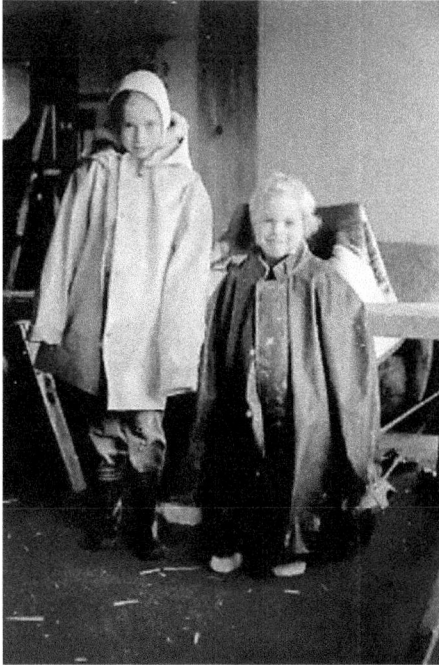

Who would dare to harm little angels, such as these?

* * *

"Tim?" It was late in the evening and the children were asleep. "I've been thinking." A repeating vision of marred babies and charred dreams flooded her mind, momentarily choking off her words.

"What have you been thinking?" Tim prompted.

"Sometimes I think it's *dangerous* for us to be living up here surrounded by so many malcontents."

There, she'd said it. She had shared her growing doubts about the place. That truthful admission made Kate feel awful. Suddenly melancholy, she knew she was letting down both her wonderful partner and their shared dream.

For a moment Tim looked at his wife with real concern. Then he gave her a mock left hook and a smile. "Oh, come on now, baby. It isn't *all* bad up here, is it?"

"About seventy-thirty, I'd say."

She elaborated. "It used to be that all our problems were of our own making. We got ourselves into spots, and we got ourselves out. Now, with all these strangers moving in, we might be less likely to freeze to death, but we're a lot more likely to get shot."

"Let's just stay away from anyone waving a gun," Tim said.

"Yeah, if we can," Kate agreed. "And let's not have a garden party this year.

Fine by me," Tim agreed.

* * *

Several delightful creatures sailed through the yard.

Gunfight at the U.A Corral

WHEN FRAMPTON'S NAME popped up in the papers in August, Tim and Kate definitely wanted to stay out of that hot potato; but it was such an interesting story that they, and most of the central Kenai, kept abreast of the situation via the *Footprint Tracker*. There was a new sequel in each weekly issue.

This beef was over horseflesh. Frampton accused the Curd brothers of sneaking in and stealing his free-grazing stallion. Greg Curd said the horse showed up at their place that spring and didn't look like anyone had fed it in ages, so he'd started feeding it and taking care of it.

When Frampton saw that the horse had grown fat and sassy, he wanted the animal returned. Curd agreed to give back the stallion, but only if Fram would pay him for the three months of horse feed.

Now this is where it got strange.

Not willing (or able?) to come up with the cash, Frampton rustled a passel of Curd's horses and hid them out in a remote corral on Upper Moose Flat. Then he demanded the return of his stallion for the return of the Curd herd. A story like this could have come right out of *Rawhide*. Needless to say, everyone was curious to know where Frampton was hiding a herd of horses, and what was going to happen next.

It made for an interesting summer.

* * *

Meanwhile, between the tree house and the twins, and running through the new sprinkler on the Peterses' lawn, that summer season zipped by. It was gone before the children ever knew what hit them.

One day, as Tim, Kate, Attie, and Brew were all squeezed into the Jeep cab, coming home from Footprint, Kate mentioned the unthinkable. "It's almost time to head back to Anchorage."

Attie stiffened. "But we don't want to leave," she said, resisting immediately.

"School will be starting soon, Attie," Kate said. That was all the children needed to know.

"But I don't like school."

"Hah!" Tim looked over at his little girl. "You told me you loved school." Now he spoke to Kate. "You guys might want to head up with me next Sunday, unless you think you can wait for one more week."

"School starts in less than two weeks. We'd better leave with you on Sunday," Kate said, nodding regretfully.

Attie figured they might be deciding her fate here. So, she spoke up again. "We could skip school."

The little girl looked pleased to offer the sacrifice.

"No, sweetie. You need to go to school, and so does Brew. Don't forget, he's starting kindergarten this year."

Attie's smile morphed into a pout. "But we love it here."

Brew followed her lead. "We love it here," he said, folding his little arms across his chest and assuming a frown almost as fierce as his older sister's.

"Your daddy and I love it here, too—especially in the summer," their mother agreed. "But the school year is starting, and we have to go."

"Why can't we go to school here?"

"And how would I get both of you to school from here?"

"You could take us on the snow-machine." Attie suggested, still intent on bending her mother's will.

The memory of one particular elasticized-bowling-ball-and-snow-machine-loaded-laundry-run incident, years ago, swung through Kate's mind. "Nope. That's out. We're going to Anchorage."

"You hate us," Brew began to whimper.

"Yes, you guessed it. That's why your daddy and I have nearly killed ourselves building this place for you: because we hate you so much."

Was she kidding? Brew couldn't tell.

Their mother quieted then but she made it clear that the decision was non-negotiable. "We all love it here, Brew. But we *aren't* staying for the winter. That's all. "

Despite their begging, as soon as Tim had left for the work week, Kate began packing.

By the time he got home the next Friday, they had everything they'd be taking with them stacked up in one corner of the living room. That night they all lay in their beds inside a half-boxed-up house that sort of felt like home and sort of didn't.

They would all be departing together on Sunday.

* * *

After they arrived in Anchorage, the new kindergartener finally agreed to relinquish his beloved baby blanket in trade for a "big boy" coat. So, right before Brew's first day of school, Kate took him to the store to pick out his new big boy winter protection.

"I like this one," Brew announced. He was strutting and twirling in a miniature black leather flight jacket he'd pulled from the rack.

"But this one looks so much warmer. See?" His mother showed him the drawstring waistband on a parka-style coat she was holding. "Won't you please try this one on for me?"

"Okay. I'll try it on," he said, obliging his mama, "but we're *getting this* one!" Clearly, Neil Brewster was developing a sense of style. Kate had to respect that.

* * *

Meanwhile, down on the Kenai, tensions over the horse-rustling issue were continuing to build. Things broke loose in early autumn.

Kate was walking past a newspaper stand, and there it was in black and white.

MAN DIES IN KENAI SHOOTOUT

A rural man was killed and two others were wounded Tuesday afternoon when the three,

who had been feuding for weeks over horses, met on grazing land and shot it out.

The ongoing dispute over stolen horses got out of control and turned into a deadly shooting on the Kenai Peninsula this week. Frampton Snyder, of Footprint, was killed after exchanging gunfire with brothers Greg and Craig Curd of Round Top Mountain.

Snyder had hidden several of the Curds' horses at the University of Alaska's Extension Service livestock corral in Moose Flat. The two brothers were attempting to retrieve the horses, which Mr. Snyder had admitted stealing in retaliation for what he claimed was the theft of his stallion. It is unknown whether a verbal argument escalated into a gun battle or—as some speculate—Mr. Snyder was lying in wait for the brothers, and he came out shooting.

Frampton Snyder died at the scene and both Curds were injured in the gunfight.

"At this time it's unlikely that anyone will be charged with Mr. Snyder's death," a local law enforcement officer said of the incident.

She fed a quarter into the box, grabbed a copy of the *Anchorage Daily News,* and rushed home to show Tim.

Kate waggled the front page at him as she entered the apartment. "Look at this!""What?"

"Fram is dead!"

"What?"

"He died in a gunfight." Kate handed him the paper. "That makes three arsons, two stabbings, two roaming rapists, and four shootings (not counting Fram's six pigs). That's a staggering ratio of residents to violent acts, isn't it? What *else* is likely to happen here on Round Top Road?"

"Hmmm." Tim was immersed in reading the stunning story. "If Fram was hiding the horses in the University of Alaska's Extension Service corral, then that would mean that the shootout wasn't far away from Victory Garden. That little rendezvous would've made a fine movie sequel: 'Gunfight at the U.A. Corral.'"

"I know you're joking. But, wow! I can't believe it." Then Kate grew somber. "I'm just glad we never got into a fight with him, or it really *might* have been 'over my dead body.' I'm not proud to admit it, but I feel a million times better, now that I know Fram is finally, *really* out of the picture. He caused a lot of trouble over the years and left a lot of manure to wash away under the bridge."

Kate did feel sorry for Ruth, though. Clearly, she had made a bad choice when she married Fram. Now she was the widowed mother of Jimmy, the convicted child molester, and stuck with Fram's name in a very small community. That couldn't be easy. Would Ruth stay in Footprint? Maybe the city might be a better place to live down your ignominy. Get lost in the crowd, so to speak.

KENAI MAN DEAD IN SHOWDOWN!

Sleeping Moose squatter, Frampton Snyder, was killed when he and two other rural residents, who had been feuding for weeks over horses, met on grazing land and the dispute led to a shootout.

Trooper J. B. Jones reported that the loose stallion situation had unfortunately gotten out of control. "Frampton Snyder exchanged gunfire with brothers Craig. and Greg Curd on Round Top Mountain. Snyder died of his wounds and both Curds were injured. The showdown came about after Snyder accused the Curds of taking his stallion, and he took their horses in retaliation. It is believed that no one will be charged in Snyder's death.

"The goal is that people don't shoot at each other," Jones said.

FOOTPRINT Weekly TRACKER

Number 37   September 20, 1987   Area weather: Rain

MAN KILLED IN GUNFIGHT!

Troopers examine the body of Frampton Snyder, a Footprint man with ties to the Sleeping Moose area who was killed Tuesday in a shootout. Brothers Craig and Greg Curd, of Round Top Mountain were wounded when an ongoing argument with Snyder over stolen horses erupted into gunfire. The showdown took place at the University of Alaska's Kenai Borough Extension Service corral on Upper Moose Flat. Evidence indicates that Snyder confronted the Curds when they came to collect their horses. This was the dramatic culmination of a month-long dispute which this paper has been covering. Snyder first told this reporter that his stallion had been stolen over the summer, but the Curds denied that allegation.

SLEEPING MOOSE BUGLE

WIDOW NOW LEFT ALONE

Recently widowed, Ruth Snyder and son Orvis will remain in Footprint after her slain

HOMER NEWS

Man is killed in gunfight

Anchorage Daily News   Wednesday, September 16, 1987

Man dies in rural shootout

By NANCY MONTGOMERY
Daily News reporter

A local man was killed and two others wounded Tuesday afternoon when the three, who had been feuding for weeks over horses, met on grazing land and shot it out.

Victoria's War

AFTER THE NEWS of the shootout, Tim and Kate decided to skip the family's mountain experience that Christmas and, instead they took the children to Hawaii for two weeks of Big Island fun. Things had just gotten too weird around Sleeping Moose. Then, they enjoyed Easter vacation with Dick and Bob in Anchorage, for the same reason.

By June, they were finally ready to head home again. Their nemesis was gone, and things should have cooled off some. At the turnoff in Sleeping Moose, the road looked good and they steamed up the hill. When they got to the bridge, the road looked so dry that they decided to try driving all the way home. This might be some kind of a record—making it up to the front door so early in June. The mood in the Gremlin was jubilant.

But their mood changed as soon as they started across the Goodmans' upper field.

At the far end, a woman stood in the middle of the road. She was pointing a rifle at them. Tim stopped the car on the dirt two-track and studied the unfamiliar figure.

She wasn't more than five-foot-tall, but she looked plenty dangerous with that rifle on her hip.

He drove the car forward slowly, and coasted to a stop a few feet away from her.

"Who are you, and what are you doing up here?" the little lady demanded, still holding the family at gunpoint.

Tim and Kate looked at each other. Who was *she?* And what had happened over the winter? Had Jason gone and gotten himself a *woman?*

"I'm Tim Peters," Tim said. "Our place is up behind here, at the end of the road."

"Oh," the road warrior said, and she lowered her weapon. "I'm Victoria. I live here with Jason, and maybe you don't know it, but you're driving through our yard." She nodded over toward Kanker's cabin. "From now on, Jason and I would like to have you find another way to get to your place."

Back when Jason Kanker was building his home so close to the right-of-way, neither he nor Tim thought it would be a problem if the two bachelors both built on the narrow knoll, as long as they kept the right-of-way free and clear. That was just common rural decency. Too bad they never shook on it, because now it looked like Victoria might want to *make* it a problem.

Was it *greed* that made people want— not only what they already had but what the other guy had as well? Yes, greed was like a cancer. And anyone could be susceptible to its ravages.

"You'll have to drive around," she said with finality.

Was she serious? "Driving around" meant going down into the flat, which was swamp land. No one could drive through that muskeg.

"We have legal access," Tim explained. "Before Neil Goodman left Alaska, he bulldozed a cut through the trees, as well as that last low section of woods beyond. It's a dedicated road. Jason knew that, when he built here. He knew we'd be driving to and from our place using this road. You can ask him."

"Believe me, I will," Victoria vowed.

But—for the time being their newest neighbor appeared to be satisfied—and she stepped back to let them pass. Tim nodded curtly, put the Gremlin in gear, and steered across the land she had just claimed as hers.

"I hope she isn't gonna be another neighbor from hell, come to replace Frampton," Kate mumbled to Tim. She could already feel a lump of dread developing under her heart.

The Peters family continued up what they firmly believed was their legal right-of-way—through the break in the trees at the top of the knoll, over the hill, and down through the last patch of mushy woods. They went right past Radley's road, and out into their own front meadow, which was bursting with lupines in bloom. Somehow, it all seemed ironic.

Over the years, Tim and Kate had tried to use diplomacy in the local road-issue politics, but now it looked like there might be some real trouble brewing. And this time, if a road war did break out, the Peterses would be in the thick of it.

Tim shook his head. "I think poor old Jason's gonna have his hands full with Victoria."

Kate said, "Dammit!"

JOURNAL ENTRY-JUNE 10, 1988—
WE'RE BACK UP ON THE MOUNTAIN AFTER
ANOTHER YUCKY, DARK WINTER IN
OUR YUCKY, DARK APARTMENT.
A FEROCIOUS NEW BEAST HAS REARED UP IN THE
NEIGHBORING FIELD: JASON'S GOT A WOMAN.
AND WHAT A WOMAN! JUST WHEN WE'VE FINALLY
GOTTEN RID OF FRAMPTON—THE NEIGHBORHOOD
PROBLEM CHILD—HERE COMES VICTORIA, READY
TO FILL IN THE VOID AND TRY TO OWN THE WORLD.
AAAACK!

The Hill of Broken Dreams

IT WAS YET *another* separation scene. Tim was leaving for work, and Kate was hanging onto the car door for one last word and a parting kiss.

"Well, I'd better go." He said, starting the Gremlin. "I guess I'll see you in a couple of weeks, then."

"*Three* weeks," Kate gently clarified. "I just hope Victoria doesn't make things difficult for us. It aggravates me that she thinks she's *allowing* us to use the road."

"You just stay up here and have fun in your garden."

"Okay, babe. I will. And you have fun up at P.S.#1." Kate leaned in through the open window to kiss him goodbye before releasing her hold on the side of the car and stepping back.

Tim drove away through the pasture, and Kate watched his rooster-tail cloud follow his progress down the mountain. When she knew Tim was safely past Victoria and her gun, she went inside the house and shut the door.

Throughout the summer, Victoria had been keeping a tight vigil on "her" knoll. Kate suspected an altercation might be coming between herself and the renegade riflewoman. If it were up to Kate, it would come in the form of a good old-fashioned—

two-women-rolling-in-the-mud "tita" fight—Hawaiian-style. Kate was twice Victoria's size, and after a decade on the mountain she was as strong as an ox. She would win through brute force.

But her adversary usually had that rifle with her, and she looked like she knew how to use it. So, instead of prodding the bull, Kate decided to ration her trips into town.

She and the children would play in their own backyard, experiencing the freedom of their own private (if somewhat diminishing) piece of wilderness. During that summer, Kate and the kids only headed down the road for their mail and grocery run once a week, weather permitting.

* * *

On Wednesday, their regular go-to-town day, they crossed Goodman's upper field as usual, and Kate was elated to see that Victoria was not at home.

But when they returned from town six hours later, Neil's beautiful field of farmable prairie had been bisected by a hastily planted line of fence posts. The new fence line ran down the middle of the two-track road, forcing vehicles over onto Butch's land and away from Jason and Victoria's place.

As she drove closer, Kate could see a nightmare vision. Each pole had a severed animal's head impaled on its top. Disgusting!

There was no other way to cross the field and reach home. They would have to drive this macabre new "Appian" way.

"Why don't you guys close your eyes for Mama while I count to ten, okay?"

They both giggled and ducked their heads. She could only hope that they weren't peeking. The sight was too impactful to ever forget. Kate counted slowly, as they passed each bloody head. "One . . . two . . . three . . ."

And then, there she was: "Vicious Victoria," beating down a row of defenseless leafy greens.

The mean-looking woman ceased her flailing to stare at them with one raised eyebrow, as if daring Kate to say something about the grotesque new installation at Jason Kanker's place.

Kate, incensed, was unable to keep mum. "What's with all the dead animal heads?"

"We don't like trespassers," the miniature-meanie snarled. "You know that." She seemed to be itching for a fight.

"These severed heads are gory. I'm asking you nicely to take them down."

"They're on *our* property," Victoria said, "so, I don't have to." The newcomer stood with hoe in hand, boots planted, glaring at the neighbors who lived up the road.

Was this about to turn into another "over my dead body" episode, like the day when Frampton first showed up? Déjà vu. The lump of concern under Kate's heart quickly morphed into a gaping sinkhole. She thought about how hard she and Tim had worked over the past decade, and now this little imp was threatening to take it all away: all the autonomy, and all the joy.

Victoria wanted
to take away
all of Kate's joy.

"Well, *gee whiz* , Vicky! If you want to get technical, this stuff of yours is *in* the legal right-of-way." Kate felt obliged to spell this out for the interloper. You *do* realize your house sits in the middle of a platted access road, don't you?"

When she heard that, Victoria looked like she would split in two. "We'll see about that," she snapped.

Diplomacy dashed, raw rage suddenly overtook Kate, and her temper flooded out like an overflowing toilet. An ugly urge roiled up out of Kate's gut and surged through her arms and down into her fists. Kate wanted to smash Victoria's face in the dirt or sit on her chest, pin her arms down, and drool into that ugly, defenseless face of hers. Or maybe she should just knock the intruder out. Who in the heck did this snippet think she was, anyway?

From deep inside, a fierce *"Lord of the Flies"* mentality overcame Kate.

Victoria didn't have her gun with her. If Kate was going to pummel the girl, this would be the perfect opportunity

The enraged settler took hold of her truck's door handle, all coiled and ready to pounce. She paused long enough to barely hear her reason whispering above the thunder of her rage, and she deliberated. Without Tim, she was the protector of these two youngsters seated beside her. A responsible parent would take her babies away from this dangerous moment. Mother Kate choked down a guttural growl, put the truck in gear, and drove her brood away from the abomination. They had groceries to unload.

When they got home, the hate filled housewife hurled herself down at the table and wrote a scathing proclamation.

She addressed it to: "Her Nastiness, Victoria the Vicious." Then she tore it up, chewed up the pieces and spat them out into a bowl. After that, she set fire to them. As the dampened wads of paper started to smoke, she was reminded of the old Kipling poem, and she found herself repeating the one line of "Der Voortrekker" that she knew by heart:

His neighbours' smoke shall vex his eyes—
their voices break his rest . . .

How true that had turned out to be.

* * *

JOURNAL ENTRY-JULY, 1988 –
TODAY'S RUN-IN WITH OUR NEWEST
NEIGHBOR IS THE LAST STRAW! I SWEAR I'VE
JUST "SEEN THE ELEPHANT," AND I'M READY TO
CALL IT QUITS.
WHEN TIM GETS HOME NEXT WEEK, I'M GOING
TO SIT HIM DOWN FOR A SERIOUS TALK
ABOUT PUTTING OUR FARM ON THE MARKET,
WHILE WE'RE ALL STILL IN ONE PIECE!
I HOPE I CAN MAKE HIM SEE
THE REASON IN THIS.

Elephants in the Wood

KATE HAD VENTURED north in 1973 because she never felt at ease in any city, even Honolulu. Influenced by Emerson's writings on transcendentalism and encouraged by Mamasan—who shared a kindred spirit—she'd headed for Alaska soon after college.

Later, when she and Tim had impulsively opted to hew their own home and raise a family out in the bush, she had pressed on faithfully beside him to help create their version of a perfect world.

After tons of intense labor, Kate had just now realized that the old ways and gentler times they'd shared with the Goodmans had departed with the Goodmans, and the vacuum left by their absence had been filling with bullies.

She continued her contemplation: *malcontents tend to gravitate to remote hollows—unpopulated, unregulated—at the end of long, rural roads, like this one here.*

Clearly, the Peterses were surrounded by some of the meanest-spirited folks in the borough, and there were very few "good guys" (i.e., Alaska State Troopers) around to protect them.

Instead of providing an opportunity for unbridled freedom, their idyllic wilderness had become a breeding ground of lawlessness and vigilantism. This reality was threatening their little homestead, their family and their dream.

The epiphany was devastating.

* * *

JOURNAL ENTRY- EARLY AUGUST
LITTLE MISS BOSSY WITH THE BIG FAT GUN JUST LET IT BE KNOWN THAT SHE'S PREGNANT, AND SHE AND JASON ARE GETTING MARRIED. SO, IT LOOKS LIKE SHE'LL BE STAYING AROUND FOR A LONG, LONG TIME.
WELL, I SAY, LEAVE IT TO HER. I'VE HAD IT!
. . . I HATE TO ABANDON MY FLOWER GARDEN— WHICH I'VE GROWN TO LOVE—
AND THE BEAUTIFUL HOUSE THAT TIM BUILT, AND THIS MAGNIFICENT FLOWER-EMBLAZONED SLOPE THAT WE'VE CALLED "HOME" FOR SO LONG.
IT'S A REAL HEARTBREAK.

That evening, Kate walked around Victory Garden, wanting to memorize every inch of its magnificence, both inside and out, because this wonderful house they had built might have to be left behind.

She stopped at her flower garden and studied a patch of forget-me-nots. They were an unmatchable blue. She loved them because they were so tiny, yet strong. They were delicate, yet they flourished in the Arctic well enough to be called the "State Flower of Alaska." Maybe they yielded to the snow the way grasses bent to the wind: living successfully through the practice of Tao.

She spoke tenderly to her periwinkle beauties. "Don't you worry, my little darlings, I'll *never* forget you, or Alaska, or the magical years we've spent on this mountain."

She plucked one delicate Forget-me-not bloom
to keep in her journal.

* * *

Earlier, in the great room, she'd traced the stains that blemished their gracious ceiling beams. Now, out in the yard she took note of the perpetually stunted birches that she had transplanted, hoping to grow a stand of trees. The futility made her chuckle bitterly. "We can't s e e m t o beat the water *o r* the moose."

Kate sighed. True, the kids were happy enough—for now—but for how long? When would the next assault bruise their tiny community? When would unexplained arson blister another family? Apparently, the stabbings and shootings were going to continue, because this *was* the wild west—at the end of the road—on the last frontier. What *had* she been expecting, *anyway?*

This mountain was a dangerous place to try to nurture a family of fruitful human beings. The odds were too heavily stacked against them. Between untameable Mother Nature and the uncivil Homo sapiens who lived nearby, the chances of raising healthy, productive children around here were getting slimmer all the time.

In Kate's mind, the day had come for them to leave the mountain behind and find a safer place to dream a new dream.

Tim would be back in a week, and she resolved to talk with him then about a new plan.

* * *

She broached the subject of moving on, as soon as the children were in bed that first night Tim was home. She described the latest incident with Victoria, to which Tim said, "Maybe everything will quiet down."

"Hah!" she snorted. "I tell you, Tim, the more this mountain fills in, the more I want to clear out."

At first, Tim rejected what he was hearing. "But we've *nearly* got things *licked*," he argued. "We've got power and a phone, and water. You've even got your flush stool in a fancy bathroom. All that's left is the road—and with all of our rigs, we've just about got *that* problem beat, too."

"Yes, but we're *never* gonna beat the "*neighbor*" problem. We had Fram for *ten years*, and now we've got *Victoria* to contend with. I don't want to stay here. It's not safe."

Tim, still not ready to cut and run, countered her argument. "Sure, it's hard here, but think of all the things a person can do in Alaska that he can't do anywhere else."

"Yeah. Like freeze to death."

"No. Seriously," he insisted.

"Okay. Seriously," Kate began to list: "A hunting, fishing, skiing bush pilot would have a pretty good time up here, I think; but Timmy, how much do you like to hunt, really?"

He thought for a moment. "Not much, I guess."

"And do you like to fish?" Kate asked.

"No."

"How about skiing?"

"Not really."

"Flying?"

"Nope."

"Okay." Then here's the question: why are we risking our lives to live up here?"

Tim looked contemplative for a moment. Then he arched his eyebrows and took a guess. "We're answering the call of the wild?"

Kate was glad that her partner still had his sense of humor. "Well, I'd say we've answered that call by now, wouldn't you? Maybe it's time to move."

She gave him a tender smile and went on lobbying. "Anna Tanner told me that she and Brian are packing it in. They're moving down to Washington State."

"Ah, that's too bad," Tim said. "I'll miss old Brian. Why do you suppose they're pulling up stakes?"

"I can think of a thousand reasons," Kate answered flatly.

After a long silence Tim said, "I guess if you really want to go, we could put the place up for sale, move outside, and start over again someplace else."

"I think I'm done with this place, my sweet. I'm tired of all the fighting up here."

Tim was listening now, so she went on. "I know this is our home, built with our own sweat and blood . . . *yours,* mostly. But short of shooting a couple of local ne'er-do-wells, I don't see what else we can do."

She looked around the big room at their hard-won accomplishment. "Victory Garden is pretty much built now. Let's let someone else take it over, and we'll go someplace new. We can begin *another* dream. After all, you said it yourself: we're *builders*, not *maintainers.*"

Tim was starting to nod along. "We'll start over again, on a *road,* this time," he vowed.

Now it was Kate who paused. "Gosh, Timber, do we have it in us to start *all* over again?"

"Sure, we do."

"I wish we could just move this house somewhere else." She conjured an image of dragging their post-and-beam palace down the narrow winding mud road. Impossible. Suddenly, the idea of living in a mobile home didn't sound so bad.

"Oh Timber, you built us such a beautiful house—"

He interrupted her. "*We* built this house, you and me *together.* Remember Kate, you were on the other end of every beam."

For a moment the lady was overcome by his sweet sentiment, but then she continued. "It's just gotten so *inhospitable* around here. Most of the folks up this road are dangerous, unpredictable, unruly bullies."

Kate thought of an old Pogo cartoon she'd once read. It said something like: "I have seen the enemy, and the enemy is us."

She contemplated the new and turbid future that she saw creeping over their formerly pristine paradise. "Given the choice," she confessed, "I preferred the howling winds of solitude to this end-of-the-road gang of thugs we have as neighbors now."

* * *

The next day, the two dispirited dreamers were sitting on the garden glider, looking at the house they had barely finished crafting, considering the evaporation of their utopian quest in the stark clarity of full daylight.

They had finally met "The Elephant," and it had turned out to be their own species.

Some humans just don't play well with others.

Kate was still trying to convince Tim to move on. "I never want to go through another winter like '79, either. And with the neighbors and all, I think it's time to go."

Tim said nothing, so she went on. "Can't we just say, 'We came; we saw; we survived?' I mean, that's a good enough story to tell, isn't it?"

Tim was shaking his head, still fighting the glacier. "But we can't just give up."

"We wouldn't be giving up. I'm saying that we should let go of this withering thread and be ready to catch the next one, when it sails by."

"But what'll people think, if we come out with our tails between our legs?"

Kate didn't miss a beat. "What'll they think if we don't come out *at all?*" She dramatized two ridiculous but entirely possible scenarios:

"'Hey, whatever happened to that Peters family? Do you remember them? I heard they all froze to death in a blizzard.' Or, 'Too bad they got caught up in that terrible gunfight. It was over a flock o' chickens, wasn't it?'"

"And besides," she concluded, "who cares what they think? And who are they, anyway?"

Tim sat motionless for a long time as his "Jeremiah Johnson" mountain man fantasy crumbled into fragments before his eyes.

Finally, he spoke. "So, you're saying 'It's time to go, sourdough?'"

"That would be my vote, yes. Lucky soldiers get to go home. After all, you came home from Vietnam, and then you met me and became a terrific husband and father. Do you think it would have been better to end up as a nice purple heart on your mother's mantle? I say we can remember the Alamo, but we don't have to die here. It's not safe to stay," she warned, again.

For Tim this would be a long slide down to the depths of heartbreak valley. But Kate was already there, and she would be ready to help him when he landed. She sat quietly and waited for her mate to catch up.

That's when Tim finally acknowledged the Elephant.

After a minute, her old "Timber" was back. "Well, at least we tried," he said at last.

"We sure did, baby."

"That's more than a lot of folks can say."

"More than a *lot* of folks can say."

Kate confirmed. The soon-to-be retired wilderness wife smiled at her man and paraphrased, "'Tis better to have reached for and missed, than never to have reached at all . . . right?"

"I guess," Tim said. He looked toward the mountain, weighing their alternatives over again as he continued his slide toward the hard landing.

"Okay, then. It's decided. If that's what you want, we'll go. We'll put up a sign at the turnoff tomorrow: For Sale—Hill of Broken Dreams."

His sarcasm stung. But Kate had, after all, just ripped out his heart. "I'm sorry, Timber. Truly sorry."

"Maybe we could go to Vermont," she suggested. "Remember how we wanted to go to Vermont?"

"I sure do. Yeah. We can go to Vermont."

"We can start a Christmas tree farm there. The kids will love it."

. . . Silence followed as Tim's usual upbeat spirit seemed to fade away completely. "Did we fail here, Kate?"

"No, sweetheart. We didn't fail. We reached out for the gold ring on this merry-go-round of life. And remember, even if we missed the grand prize, we still got one heck of a good ride out of it."

He smiled at that. "We did have some good times up here, didn't we?"

"We had the *best* of times," Kate agreed softly.

"Maybe we'll come back to see this place again one day," Tim said.

"Maybe," Kate said. "But not for a long time. Maybe we can come back when it doesn't hurt."

Tim doubted that day would ever come. If they left, they might never return. It was over.

Resigned at last, he switched gears. They would make the most of these last days in the garden.

"Speaking of merry-go-rounds, where are the kids?" he asked.

"They're down at the tree house."

"Hmmm. You don't say. Do you need any *tilling* done around here?"

Kate shot him a sly grin. "Well, I do have a couple of things I want to show you in the greenhouse."

"Lead the way," her mate said.

She untied her shoes and slipped them off. "Let's go in barefoot. I've let the fireweed grow tall around the outside, so it's very pink and private in there."

Tim followed after her, like a horse drawn to the sweet smell of oats. Then Kate opened the door to her secret garden and let him come in.

* * *

That evening they sat side-by-side in their view chairs, gazing out at the fading gloaming. Tim finally spoke, sounding defeated. "I guess we set our anchor in the wrong port, my dear."

Kate didn't feel much better, but she would try to be strong for him. "Well, I'll agree that it's one heck of a disappointment, the way things turned out . . . but, ever onward."

* * *

The next morning the parents broke the news to their children, who both flew into tantrums and ran outside. They continued howling out there like injured wolf pups, while their parents began to put the new plan into action.

Ignoring their outrage, Kate got out the paint, and lettered eight big words onto a board Tim had dug out of the scrap pile.

FOR SALE

HOUSE ON 40 ACRES

GREAT VIEW

Phone / info. available at Sleeping Moose Post Office

She added an arrow, and in smaller letters she put contact information. This way, potential buyers could call to inquire without driving all the way up the road, although Kate knew it would take *seeing the view* to make the sale.

— 6 —

Kansas or Bust!

Tossing Out the Pump Organ

AFTER BREAKFAST, EVERYONE piled into the M-37 and drove out to post the "For Sale" sign down in Sleeping Moose.

The children hadn't taken the news well.

To help smooth things over, Tim let Attie steer the truck down to Sleeping Moose and Brew would pilot it back home. The little ones forgot all of their resentment as they swerved the M-37 around and through the muddy track.

Kate was watching the road unfold like origami in front of them. "What'll we do with this wonderful old truck?" she asked Tim.

"We'll sell it," he said.

"I have to say, the smell inside this truck is one of my all-time favorites. Why don't we take it with us? It would look great in the driveway in Vermont."

"How long would it take us to drive the Alcan Highway at 35 mph?" Tim quizzed. "And how many gas cans would we have to carry in the back? No, Katherine, m'lady. When we go, the truck stays—just like almost everything else on the mountain."

"Are we leaving our two view chairs and your mother's marble-topped table behind?"

At the mention of these three pieces Tim's resolve softened. "Okay, we can take those," he agreed.

Kate thought of her cast iron skillets, looking happy in the hand-hewn kitchen, hanging from their beam. Yes, they would have to stay. And her snowshoes, too, she supposed, which made Kate sad. Besides Tim and the kids, those snowshoes were probably her best friends on the mountain.

She was having difficulty parting with everything: her dishes, the frying pans, the bed that had been a wedding gift from Mamasan, the antique dressers, desk and tables, Elsie's couch and chair, all those lovely glass doorknobs, the Skidoos, the Weasel, the Jeep, the shop full of tools, and their nostalgically aromatic Dodge Power Wagon. And, of course her wildflower garden would stay.

"Once you haul it up the mountain, it belongs to the mountain," Tim uttered the dictate for the umpteenth time. If they'd been Forty-Niners he'd have been telling her to toss out the pump organ. It was like the day Elsie had to leave behind *her* dream and all of her canning.

When the pilgrims left, they would be leaving not only the mountain and most of their belongings, but a huge part of their lives as well. Maybe even the richest part of their lives.

But the family would be safe, and that was the most important thing. Everything else was just *stuff*, she told herself again.

Suddenly Kate laughed as she pictured their Jeep, its headlights held in place with underpants. "It'll take a mighty special person to love our rigs the way we do."

* * *

On the next sunny day, Kate climbed up on top of the shop roof to paint an advertisement up there. September was moose hunting season, which meant an especially busy sky overhead. She painted the letters four feet high, like the big tobacco signs on barns of old.

"It reminds me of Minnesota or something," Tim said as he inspected her work.

"Have you ever been to Minnesota?"

"No. But I've seen pictures."

"If we drove the M-37, we could see Minnesota for ourselves: take a long, slow look," Kate hinted. She surely did love that truck, and she knew Tim did, too.

* * *

Summer, 1988—Dear Mamasan,

Thanks for the encouraging words about our decision to change our life direction. Tim still looks a little shell-shocked; but he says he's willing to move on, so I'm loading up the wagon and getting us out while the barn door is open.

The hard part will be finding someone to buy the farm—since we're a little off the beaten path. We'll be lucky to get any kind of an offer at all. But we put a notice down at the post office and a sign at the turnoff, and I painted "FOR SALE" in huge letters on the shop roof, since we get a lot more float planes than cars coming by. Maybe we'll catch ourselves a well-heeled hunter.

Love, Kate

P.S. Any way you slice it, this extraction is going to hurt, though.

* * *

"I saw a picture in the paper the other day," Tim was saying. "It looked like *The Grapes of Wrath*. The road south is clogged with cars from here to Canada. I guess people are just throwing their keys on the floor and driving away."

Kate frowned at his news. "That's not good. Who's gonna want to buy our farm, with houses being given away all over the state?" After searching her brain, she came up with a novel suggestion. "Maybe we can get someone in Japan to buy it. They've got the money these days. My brother's old roommate lives there. Maybe he could place an ad in the paper for us."

Tim shrugged. "Maybe. It's worth a try, I guess . . . Okay, why don't you put something together? We'll send up a flare, and see if anyone responds."

Kate quickly worked up a book full of photos, along with a carefully worded ad, and she sent the whole package off to her brother's friend in Tokyo.

Their contact called back from Japan a week later.

"Are you sure you want all this information in the ad? You know, things are pretty expensive here these days."

"How expensive is "expensive?""

"Well, it's two-fifty a line for one night: or a thousand dollars a line for one week."

At ten pages of photos and a detailed description of their rustic jewel, Kate could see what he meant. "Oh. Well, in that case, let's trim it to one line and run it for one night, just to get a feel for the market. Would you mind doing that?"

"Will do," her friend had said.

They wired him the money, and he ran the ad—but no one from Japan ever inquired.

* * *

One week later they had their first nibble from the sign down in Sleeping Moose.

Kate caught sight of the vehicle the second it emerged from the woods, and she estimated they would have thirty seconds to prepare the place for a good first impression.

"Kids, run and make your beds! Someone's coming up the road! We've got to whip this place into shape!"

The Jeep stopped at the bottom of the field, and two figures got out. They stood there for quite some time, just looking at the house. Kate, mistress of a hopefully immaculate household, was sizing them up.

Would these be the ones?

She waited and watched. Then, when they got back into their car, turned around, and drove away, Kate called off the drill. "Never mind, guys. They left."

Wisely, Kate decided to walk down the hall to see how well the children had done with their room-straightening assignment.

They hadn't done well at all. She stood in the doorway, hands on her hips.

"Okay, guys. I know it's a pain, but we have to have this house ready to show off at the drop of a hat. We never know when someone is going to come up the road and want to see our place. We're looking for the perfect person to love our home as much as we do. If it's messy, they won't like what they see and they'll turn around and leave."

Attie and Brew gave each other a desperate look as their mother continued. "Here's what we're gonna have to do. We're going to keep this place tidy all the time. Every minute. We'll have to keep our beds made, our toys picked up, and the toilet flushed."

"Ah gee, Mom," the two complained.

Then Attie piped up. "We don't wanna leave."

"I know, honey. Believe me. None of us wants to go. But it's time to move now. Your daddy and I both wish things had turned out differently, but this is the way it is."

Kate couldn't think of anything else to say, so she shrugged her shoulders. "You'll love our new home just as much as this one."

"Can we have a tree house?" Brew wanted to know.

"Sure, you can." Kate gave each child a hug. "Now let's promise to keep our beds made, and the place picked up, okay?"

"Okay," the two youngsters promised. Then they got dressed and took off for Bobby and Benny's—leaving dirty clothes and toys lying everywhere in their wake.

She watched her darlings trot away. "This is *not* going to be an easy sale," the desperate housewife mumbled to herself.

* * *

JOURNAL ENTRY

MORE INTERVIEWS AT GUNPOINT!

NOW, THERE'S A GUY NAMED STEVE WHO'S RENTING THE RADLEY PLACE. TIM JUST MET HIM. HE TOTES A GUN AND—LIKE VICTORIA—HE WANTS TO KNOW WHO'S PASSING BY "HIS" PLACE, AND WHY.

BETWEEN VICTORIA AND HER GUN, AND STEVE AND HIS GUN, DRIVING HOME COULD BECOME A LIFE AND DEATH ISSUE EVEN IN GOOD WEATHER!

LIFE ON THIS MOUNTAIN ISN'T A CELEBRATION OF LIBERTY ANYMORE. INSTEAD OF ENJOYING ULTIMATE FREEDOM EARNED THROUGH PERSONAL RESPONSIBILITY, WE'RE CARRYING LIFE AND DEATH RESPONSIBILITIES WHILE EXPERIENCING VIRTUAL IMPRISONMENT

. . . AND I HAVE TO KEEP MY CLOTHES ON AT ALL TIMES!

I CAN'T STAND IT!

* * *

Dear Grandma Tutu,

We've still got our big sign posted down at the turnoff, and a smaller one at the bridge. It hasn't rained for several days, so the road is drivable. Cross your fingers for us.

Bill and Pat O'Leary had their house rebuilt after the fire, and they just sold it to a couple returning from the oil fields in Saudi Arabia. The buyers paid cash right out of a suitcase in the trunk of their car! I hope we have equally good luck. We shall see. Thank you so much for all your emotional and financial assistance to us. It really helps.

More later. Fingers crossed.

Love, KTAB

For Sale: Hill of Broken Dreams

Gold Rush

THEY'D ONLY HAD two lookers come all the way up to the house so far. A father and son pair from California had gone through the place and said they liked it. But they hadn't called back.

The house was neat and all the beds were made. It was a clear, sunny Saturday—prime real estate weather—and Kate was watching the spot where their road came out of the woods.

She saw the silver touring sedan the second it cleared the last tree. "Tim, here comes a fish. Let's see if we can reel 'im in."

Both she and Tim stood watching through the window as the perspective buyers approached. This car had already bounced through six miles of woods and cleared two gun-toting "gatekeepers," and now nothing stood between its occupants and the priceless view except those last few bumps and a couple of minor grinds. Kate wanted to make her best presentation ever. By the time these folks reached the house she would be ready to throw open the door and smile wide for them.

"Remember the day we first pulled up at the Goodmans' Quonset hut?" she asked Tim. "Neil was probably pretty excited to see us pop over the hill, too."

Eventually the car pulled to a stop beside the woodshed, and a middle-aged woman sporting bright red hair climbed out of the passenger's side. She instantly reminded Kate of Miss Kitty from *Gunsmoke*. In fact, they could have been kin, except Miss Kitty hadn't worn glasses.

The woman walked out onto the front lawn and seemed to be raving about the view. When she yelled to her companion to get out of the car and join her, he obliged.

After an eternity, the woman finally turned to look toward the house and began prodding her partner toward the front door.

Tim and Kate went outside to meet them. They all shook hands, and they spent another few minutes looking at the view. Then the woman asked for a tour, and Kate happily obliged.

She gestured toward the wildflower garden, and then took them inside through the famous front door. (Kate didn't describe its installation to these strangers. No need to tell everyone their secret.)

First, the four stood in the great room and Kate told them about hewing the beams. Then she followed up with a full tour of the house, upstairs and down.

She saved the bathroom for last. When this spitting-image of Miss Kitty's cousin saw *that* room, she started to get excited, grabbed her manfriend's hand and squeezed it tight.

"Show them the sock, Freddie."

The tour ended back in the great room, where the visitors walked over to stand in front of the picture window and gaze again at the perfect view. The woman kept whispering into her companion's ear while Kate and Tim watched at a discreet distance. From where Kate stood, this woman definitely seemed interested.

After another extra-fervent whisper, the man looked at Tim and inquired about a mortgage on the place.

"No mortgage," Tim answered. "We built the whole thing out-of-pocket."

That made the man smile, even though the woman was squeezing his arm like a pressure cuff.

Another whispered discussion followed. Looking up, the man asked, "What would you take for the whole thing?"

"One fifty," Tim said. "That's for the house and forty acres."

Tim and Kate had talked this part over many-a-time, and had finally decided to let it go for less than they felt it was worth. Given Alaska's current "bust" economy, one hundred fifty thousand seemed acceptable.

The man spoke again. "So, you're asking a hundred fifty thousand for the whole lot?"

"That's right. We think that's a fair price. There's a lot of sweat equity in the place."

The man looked at Tim for a bit, then he whispered something to his woman, excused himself and went out to their car. When he returned, he was holding what looked like a sock full of marbles.

"My little woman here likes the place," he said. "So, here's what I'm prepared to offer: I'll give you one hundred thousand in gold nuggets, right now" (he began pouring rocks out of the sock), "if you'll agree to walk away from here today, and leave everything just the way it is."

Kate stared down at the irregular lumps in his hand. The lima-bean-sized rocks *looked* like gold. They were gold-colored and lumpy, but sort of smooth, like a half-polished river rock. Even if they *were real*, neither she nor Tim had any idea what that handful of nuggets would be worth.

After the man had waited for what he thought was long enough, he gave the clueless couple another option, "Or I'll pay you ninety percent of spot value on day of sale."

What did that mean? Kate was bewildered. Things were happening way too fast. And besides, who did he think he *was*, demanding that they be out by sundown? Kate was starting to resent this man's arrogance.

The imminent sale *already* didn't have Kate feeling overjoyed, and when she saw the woman sizing up her cast iron frying pans, she felt almost violated.

"Well?" The man was impatient for an answer.

"I suppose you'll be wanting our underwear, too?" the flustered saleslady asked. The man didn't catch her scantily-clad sarcasm.

"We'll take the whole works," he repeated.

"Well, we'll need to think about your terms for a while. Why don't you give us your number, and we'll call you when we've made up our minds," Tim said. He was trying to wrap up the meeting before Kate exploded.

"We want your answer *now* : before we leave here today," the buyer insisted.

Was this guy crazy? Or was he was just acting out the whole thing so he could make his honey happy and still hold onto his gold? That was possible, Kate supposed.

She stepped over to stand close to Tim. They weren't going to let this guy or his puffy-haired strumpet evict them from the home they'd built with their own four hands. No way!

Tim looked at Kate. Her face said No, as clearly as if she had it painted on her nose. And he felt the same. This was an easy decision.

"Well then, no thanks," Tim said. "I believe we'd prefer to hold out for a better offer."

After Tim gave them his answer, every drop of available blood surged up into the redhead's face. "Well!" the now-scarlet woman harrumphed. "Freddie, we're leaving. I'll be waiting for you out in the car."

She did a heel spin and started to trounce out through the side door. But she couldn't figure out how to open the one-of-a-kind spring-lever handle. So, she stood motionless and waited for Tim to open the portcullis for her.

He threw the latch and, without missing another beat, she continued her emphatic departure, hurling the door wide and stomping down the steps into the woodshed. At the bottom, she turned and wove her way between the snow-machine and the firewood and flounced out into the sunshine. Storming out to the silver sedan, she wrenched open the door handle, flung her large body inside, slammed the door shut, and sat silently waiting for her prospector boyfriend.

Before he left, Fred stopped to warn the two settlers. "You're gonna regret this decision. Once we're gone, we're gone. I doubt you'll get another offer as good as this one. Not *these* days." Tim and Kate remained stoic, so Fred gave a snort and exited through the front door. Ten seconds later they were pulling away.

"Well, babe, there goes our big chance." Tim said, as they watched their golden prospects jolt away through the field.

"They wanted *everything!*" Kate said. "I actually feel sick."

They watched the fancy car jerk around the bend and barge into the woods. When nothing was left of that disturbing visit but a cloud of dust, Kate scoffed. "Just look at the way he drives. He never would have taken care of the place. And she wasn't the least bit interested in my wildflower garden, either."

"They weren't the ones. That's all. The right person will come along. You'll see," Tim said. ". . . But we *will* have to be ready to leave just about *everything* behind, when we do go."

They had labored so hard to get every item up to their home. Kate began to feel melancholy. "Anyway, let's not dwell on that stuff right now. School starts soon. If we don't sell the place this summer, we'll try again next year."

Deus ex Machina

Deus ex machina—A mechanical device used in Greek and Roman drama to lift the protagonist up off the stage and out of an impossible situation. This introduction of a deity at the end of the play was sometimes the only way to resolve a supremely tangled plot.

Webster, II New Riverside University Dictionary

"NO ONE IS buying anything in Alaska right now, that's the problem," Tim was saying. "I think we should put an ad in the paper and see if we can at least *rent* the place out. Maybe in a year or two the economy will start to bounce back and we'll have better luck selling it—so let's find a renter, if we can, and see what happens after that."

"I hate the idea of renting out our farm."

"I doubt that anyone will come forward, but it might save on taxes if we can claim it as a rental."

"Okay, sweetheart," Kate sadly agreed. "I'll put something in the paper as soon as we get back to Anchorage."

* * *

They were holed up in Anchorage for what would, hopefully, be their last long, dark winter. As Kate composed the ad, she tried to move aside the sadness of the situation by thinking about living in Vermont, or Hawaii, or Kansas, or anywhere but Round Top Mountain. It sort of worked.

She called the paper and placed an ad offering to rent their house to the first stranger who came along. The whole process tore at her, but she went through the steps, fed her words into some kind of an electronic system, and got her blurb submitted to the Sunday want ads in the Anchorage paper. Kate knew that no one would respond. Victory Garden was just too remote. This was a "Hail Mary" play, for sure.

* * *

On Monday morning, Kate was alone in the apartment, trying yet another avenue to get them out of their predicament. She had been reading a book about visualizing one's desires into reality, and she was trying to picture signing over the deed to their place. She and Tim and a man were sitting in a professional's office. There was a third man standing between them. He was wearing a tie, and it was his office, and . . . and . . . Kate was stuck right there. She couldn't come up with enough detail to complete her vision.

"I've tried everything I can think of to get us out of here. I can't do any more." She threw out her empty hands toward the sky. "I need some help, here."

"Help!" she wailed her wish loudly, an earnest plea tumbling out of her. It exploded up from somewhere deep within.

* * *

Brr-ring. Brr-ring. Brrr-ring

Less than a minute after she'd spontaneously blurted out that earnest and completely unceremonious prayer, the phone started ringing. Startled, Kate went down the hall and lifted the receiver.

"Hello?"

"Hi. I'm calling about the ad you have in the paper."

"Ad?" For a moment, she couldn't think of what ad he meant.

"Your house on the Kenai that's for rent."

Ah yes. *That* ad! It was all flooding back now.

"Is it still available?" he was asking.

"Yes. It is," she heard herself saying.

"How much are you asking?"

She and Tim had never discussed a rental rate, since they really hadn't believed anyone would call. Kate grappled to calculate a reasonable price, and said the first number that came to mind. "We're asking six fifty a month," and she immediately second-guessed herself. *Was that too high? Should I have said four hundred?*

"That sounds good," the fellow was saying.

What? He wasn't hanging up on her? He was still interested?

"When could I see it?" Kate was still trying to get her gears in place. This caller wanted to *see* Victory Garden. He wanted to know when he could see the farm!

"Well," she began slowly, giving herself

time to think, "we can be down there next Saturday. Would you want to see it then?"

"Next Saturday sounds great. How do I get there?" The caller was guiding the dazed woman onto a freeway and into the fast lane of realty rentals.

She stumbled along. "Let's see. You take the Sterling Highway south to Sleeping Moose, which is the first settlement after Cooper Landing. Take the road that goes up the hill on the right. It's the dirt road directly across the highway from the post office. You follow that road for about two miles. Then take a left across a little bridge, and go another four miles up through some woods to a big field. Go across the field and down one last hill and through the woods—"

And that's how far she got before the would-be renter jumped in.

"Wait a minute! Did you have your place on the market for sale this summer?"

Darn it. He'd recognized their plight. "Yes," the new landlady admitted, knowing the jig was up.

"Oh, wow! We loved your house! My dad and I were up to see your place. Do you remember showing it to us?"

"Uhhh" . . . They must have been the ones who'd *ooh-ed* and *ahh-ed* but never came back.

Luckily, the caller was so excited that he picked up the conversation without waiting for her answer. "When we got back to California, we talked it over and decided we wanted to buy your farm, but by then we'd lost your phone number. I'm back in Anchorage now and I—just this minute—picked up the Sunday paper and saw your ad."

Kate was speechless. When she'd been baptized earlier that spring, the pastor had told her that God would meet her at the font. Was this it, then? Was she meeting God, at last?

"I wonder," the fellow continued, "is the place still for sale?"

You could have bowled her over with a feather. If ever there had been a *deus ex machina* moment, this was one—and it was *real* .

Well . . . yes, it is, she heard a woman inside her skin speak the incredible words.

"Good! I'll be down on Saturday. See you then." And the friendly voice was gone.

The receiver still hung in Kate's hand as she deciphered what had just happened. Did she believe in miracles? Probably not. But maybe?

"That was *totally amazing!*" Kate whispered to the empty kitchen. Still an agnostic, but maybe also a mystic, she gently hung up the phone and said a humble "thank you," to whatever force seemed to have intervened on their behalf.

* * *

When Tim came home, Kate described the strange occurrence: her unplanned prayer, followed by the miraculous and confounding phone call.

Tim listened to her strange story, but he was mostly excited about the part where the guy wanted to buy the farm.

That evening they held a family pow-wow to talk about where they might want to go after they left Alaska. Tim voted for Prince Edward Island, his ancestral home, and Attie said she'd go wherever her daddy went. Brew didn't have an opinion, since he only knew of Anchorage and Sleeping Moose. Kate said she wanted to try some place warmish and kind of normal—like maybe the Midwest—and Brew said, "Okay."

They all went to bed that night with visions of new and wonderful pasture lands dancing in their heads.

* * *

"Timber?"

"Hmm?"

He was sound asleep. Kate rolled over and gave him a little shake.

"Timmy, I really think our next adventure should be in Kansas."

Tim laughed at the notion.

"I'm not kidding," Kate said. "We should think about moving to Kansas."

"Kansas? What's in Kansas?"

"I don't know. I'm not even sure exactly where it is, but if it's mostly farm country, that means it's not real crowded: just enough hard-working souls around to scare away the weirdos. I want our children to grow up in a nice quiet place, with a porch swing and all the peace that goes along with it."

"Hmmm." Tim closed his eyes and listened to her soothing drone as she went on and on, describing her vague impression of Kansas.

"I hear they have fireflies, and robins that yank up big, stretchy worms after a good rain. And cows—oh, beautiful cows. And wonderful old barns. And nice people who would make us want to bring out the coffee pot, and not the shotgun. And baby chicks wouldn't have to arrive by mail. Maybe I'd even find a spot where I could pee out under the stars. And there would be lakes so warm that you could actually jump into one on a hot August afternoon."

Tim's mind finally engaged. "Kate, if you suddenly found yourself sitting alone out on a wide open plain someplace in Kansas Territory, and it was two hundred years ago, and all you had was the clothes on your back, what's the first thing you'd do?"

Obviously, he wasn't taking her seriously. Kate sighed and then ended the conversation. "If it was a sweltering-hot August afternoon, I'd jump in a lake! Go back to sleep. I'll tell you my idea tomorrow."

A Salute to the Road Grader

OVER THE NEXT couple of weeks, they packed up Tim's mother's marble-top table and the view chairs and a few selected items and shipped them off to Kansas City.

A thousand "lovies" that hadn't made the cut would remain behind in the silent house, waiting for their new master to arrive. Everyone was sad, and Brew was crying.

His mommy tried to calm him. "Don't worry, Brew. We can gather new lovies when we get to Kansas. You'll see. We'll fix up a nice little nest to live in, and fill it with lovies. I promise."

Somehow, her promise made Brew grow even more pensive. At last he asked, "Are we really gonna live in a nest?"

Kate smiled at the literal interpretation. "No, sweetie. We'll have a house. Everything will be just fine."

They said goodbye to all the "lovies."

When all was in order, they bade farewell to most of their worldly goods and resolutely headed away for good.

As they drove down Round Top Road, Brew's little head barely peeked out above the edge of the window, and he watched wide-eyed as they passed the familiar landmarks he would not see again.

Skirting the old wooden road grader for the very last time, Tim slowed down and saluted the icon of the trail, lying half-buried in its muddy grave. Kate sighed, and Attie and Brew watched as the Gremlin's slithering tires splattered fresh mud onto it.

"I've got to give Neil and Elsie a lot of credit," Tim told Kate. "They battled this road for nearly twenty years."

"Yes, but they didn't have a lot of disgruntled neighbors to deal with," Kate reminded him. "I love the woods and the flowers and the skies, and I don't even mind the snow," she continued. "Mud's still a pain, but mostly I just don't like the people who live at the *end* of this road. They're scary."

She thought some more. "I guess I preferred the howling winds of solitude to this knot of cantankerous cowboys who've come looking to hide out at the end of a long rural road."

Kate looked up as they approached the area Frampton Snyder had ruled. He had squatted by the bridge for a decade, showing total disregard for the law and defiling the natural beauty of his surroundings without compunction. His extended stay had been both lawbreaking and heartbreaking.

The woods would heal eventually, but Kate and Tim wouldn't be there to see it happen. They'd had enough, and they were moving on.

Encounter with a Bearded Lady

NEAR THE BRIDGE, two travelers appeared from around the bend. A man was walking and leading a paint horse with someone riding on the pony's back.

When they got closer Kate could see that the man had braids that reached almost to his waist, and the woman—for her long dress and bobbing bosom made it obvious that she *was* a woman—the woman on that horse *had a full beard!*

A complete set of whiskers shot out unchecked from her upper lip, chin, cheeks and neck. Kate's first thought was, *Whoa, Nelly! This could only happen here.*

Tim rolled to a stop beside the unusual pair. The man nodded his head respectfully before speaking. "Hello. My wife and I are looking for a place to settle. They say we might find some place up this road where we could set up our teepee."

It was hard not to stare. Were they a couple of dropouts from a traveling carnival? Or were they simply two idealists looking to create their own version of a perfect world?

That's what Tim and Kate had tried to do, but their own Emerson-inspired farming experiment had fizzled. Would these two be able to succeed, where they had not?

If a woman was ever going to be able to let her beard grow without suffering social repercussions, it would probably be in a place like this: remote and tucked away. But Kate doubted that the antisocial types at the end of the road would embrace such an idiosyncratic lady with open arms. Someone sporting such an anomaly might need to find a place even *less* populated, if she wanted to live in peace.

Tim shrugged. "You can try asking further up," he said, "but neighbors back here probably won't take kindly to strangers setting up any kind of a teepee."

The young man looked more than a bit disappointed, but he said, "Thank you," and continued leading the steed up the road and into the backwoods.

Tim drove away. He rolled the Gremlin across the bridge and turned right, headed for Sleeping Moose, and civilization beyond.

Kate began ruminating over their last encounter in the bush.

Why didn't the woman shave? Why didn't she make more of an effort to fit in? Kate had to admit that even she— who wanted everyone to love everyone— might have struggled to embrace a woman who so openly displayed her hirsutism.

For several miles the transcendentalist wrestled mentally with the realities of both community interactions and human relationships. Was it instinctive to shun those who differed from the herd? Most animals probably did so. But with the ability to reason, shouldn't people be able to accept others, regardless of their appearance?

Was *she* able to see past the personal choices of others and to accept them, no matter how different their looks or beliefs? She had her doubts.

Sad as it seemed, Kate concluded that Emerson's (and Mamasan's idea of utopia would never be attainable, as long as human beings were involved.

A Good Way to See It

"YUP, MAMASAN, WE'RE leaving tomorrow, headed for Kansas City." Kate was calling from their nearly empty apartment in Anchorage.

"Katie dear, I'm sorry things didn't work out better for you two up there."

The disappointed idealist gave a little snort. "Well, it has been a pretty bitter pill to swallow, all right. But I'm going to try to believe that it was still worthwhile. For one thing, we've seen, done, and lived something that most others only dream of."

"That's for sure," her mother agreed.

After a pause, Kate asked the older woman, "Do you remember when I first told you that we had decided to homestead in Alaska, and you said that we were 'going to see the elephant?'"

"No. Did I?"

"Yes, you did. Anyway, I didn't know what you meant, back then. But now I've done my research. It turns out that 'seeing the elephant' has both bad and good connotations. It's up to each of us to *choose* how we want to view a disappointing life experience like this one. I found an old story that reminds me to feel *joyful,* even though things didn't turn out the way we'd hoped. It was still a great adventure."

Kate paused, and then went on. "Have you ever heard the story of the farmer who longed to see that exotic creature known as the 'elephant'?"

"No, I haven't. Why don't you tell it to me?" her mother said.

"Okay. Well, back in the 1800s there was this old farmer who drove his horse drawn cart full of vegetables into town to sell at the market. That's when he heard that a circus was coming, and that the circus parade would be passing by in just a few minutes. The procession was to be led by an elephant!

"Now, this fellow had heard about the strange and exotic animal that came from the other side of the world, and he had always wanted to see one, but he'd never had the chance.

"As I've said, he was old, and he figured he might never have another opportunity like this, so he left the marketplace and drove his wagon straight through town to find a spot on the parade route. There he parked his horse and wagon in a sliver of shade right beside the road and waited for the largest living creature on earth to come by.

"After a while, here came the parade, and it was being led by the biggest animal he could have imagined. This beast was the size of a small barn, and it swayed as it walked, like it was fighting off moonshine.

"The old farmer could hardly contain his excitement as the massive animal came closer and closer to him. The ground shook as each huge foot landed, and soon it was so close that the old man could see the hairs on its kneecaps and smell the peanuts on its breath.

"Frightened, his farm horse jumped sideways, toppling the cart and dumping his whole week's-worth of tomatoes and cantaloupes into the mud."

Kate paused, and Mamasan responded sympathetically, as almost anyone would.

"Oh, that's too bad."

"That's just what the farmer's friend said," Kate agreed.

Then she went on with her story. "After he'd collected his horse and righted his wagon, he disposed of the mangled produce at a pig farm and headed home. That night his friend came over to console him. 'I heard about your accident this morning. That's too bad: a lot of hard work, and nothing to show for it.'

"And here's the part that I like," Kate said, going on. "The old farmer told his friend, 'Shucks, that weren't nothin' I can't get over.' And then he smiled, picturing again that thrill of a lifetime. 'I'm just thankful I got the chance to see such a rare and mighty sight, my friend. For I have *seen the elephant*, and ain't *nothin'* likely to ever top that!'"

A long pause floated across the ocean. "Well, that sounds like a good way to look at it," Mamasan said eventually.

"I'm just glad we came to Alaska when we did," Kate continued. "It was a lot of hard work, and I doubt we would have survived if we'd been much older. Bush pioneering is surely a young man's sport."

"Well then, I'm happy you took the opportunity when it presented itself," Mamasan said. "I guess if you want to experience an adventure, you have to go while the going is good. Seize the moment, as it were."

"The funny thing is, we didn't even know we were embarking on an adventure. We just thought we'd found a beautiful place to live a wonderful life. Tim and I think of ourselves as a couple of nineteenth-century romantics who were born a hundred years too late. He wanted to build his own house, and I wanted to live a pure and simple lifestyle." She laughed. "Boy, was I mistaken about the *simple* part! But you never know 'til you try, I guess."

There was another pause before her mother spoke again. "But why *Kansas*, Katie girl? Haven't you heard? That's 'Tornado Alley' over there. Why don't you come back to Hawaii, where the living is easy?"

"Mama," Kate sweetly responded, "why would we want to come back to Hawaii when we haven't seen *Kansas* yet?"

At that, Mamasan was silent. Why damp their brightly shining spirits?

Attie and Brew, Kate and Tim at home on the range.

Epilogue

AFTER MEETING THE elephant in the bush, and subsequently emerging from the woods, Tim and Kate Peters embraced a tamer, safer, and for the most part, easier life down in the Lower Forty-Eight.

Attie and Brew eventually forgave their parents for leaving Alaska, and they both grew up to be fine individuals.

Although they never did get to that farm in Vermont,

Tim and Kate

lived happily ever after.

The End

Conclusions from a Pioneer's Odyssey

THIS STORY WAS about two romantics' transcendental quest for Truth, Goodness and Beauty: and they were bound to be disappointed with the way it ended. It was sad to see the spot where the moose once slept—that perfect piece of untainted wild—being inundated by individuals who enacted their own idea of justice because they lived at the end of the road. Chasers of dreams deserve a happy ending, so my task as a recorder of this particular history is to reveal some sweet wisdom bought with bitter disappointment. Make lemonade out of lemons, as it were.

Now, some might say that my parents were driven away by all the hardships encountered when living in the bush, but until the day we left, my dad believed that they "nearly had things licked," and he wasn't inclined to give up. He only left the mountain because he loves my mother, and she really wanted to go.

"It's not safe," Kate had said. "If the weather doesn't kill us, one of the neighbors probably will."

Things hadn't turned out the way my parents had hoped or expected, and—in the end—it was the people, not the extremes of nature, that drove them away.

Disillusioned and disenchanted, they had disengaged from that particular dream.

* * *

The path of life tends to be uneven and unpredictable. But Tim and Kate were a well-matched team of oxen pulling together in a double yoke, and they would be fine. Between my dad's faith in his abilities, and my mom's imaginative flair, this road of theirs would etch out some great nostalgia, wherever it led.

To sum things up, here's what I know about the neighbors who lived on our road: today, more than half of them are dead or in jail, and most of the couples (including Jason and Victoria) are divorced. I think the Tanners and my parents, alone, saw the elephant and moved back to civilization before any great ill befell them.

Three unresolved issues persist.

Long ago my parents had to let go of the arson question: Who set those fires, and why? Back then, there were rumors, and my parents had their suspicions; but no one was ever arrested. The fact is, some mysteries go unsolved.

Another troublesome topic, one that still elicits sharp exchanges at the end of Round Top Road, is road access or denial of road access. That's a battle in which rifles still rule. In 2016, Victoria's son called my parents, all the way from Alaska. He claimed he was being denied access to the hunting lands that started behind our old place. What a reversal of fortune! Regardless, my mother thinks that bickering over a country road for three decades is stupid enough to make a person want to spit.

Finally, there remains the mystical enigma for which my mother has no definitive answer: Was there a divine force involved in the seemingly-miraculous sale of Victory Garden? To this day she doesn't know what to believe.

[Please feel free to speculate right along with her, for the ability to contemplate one's motivations and to seek answers to the unanswerable is a singularly human, if overrated, gift.]

Taking a Transcendentalist's Path

"Enter ye that have leisure and a quiet mind, who earnestly seek the right road."

—Henry David Thoreau, Walden, 1854

"Trust thyself: every heart vibrates to that iron string."

—Ralph Waldo Emerson, Self-Reliance, 1841

❁

Seeing the Elephant

This "was a term used by American explorers, pioneers, adventurers, gold miners and wagon train emigrants to describe the existential reckoning with one's own limits when encountering the hardships of their chosen path. Quite often, 'seeing the elephant' causes even the bravest among us to abandon the dream, and retreat to a more mundane, somewhat safer, and far more comfortable enclave of civilized society."
—Wikipedia, 2015

"I lived alone, in the woods, a mile from any neighbor, in a house which I had built myself, . . . I lived there two years and two months. At present I am a sojourner in civilized life again."
—Thoreau

"Talk with a seaman of the hazards to life in his profession and he will ask you, 'Where are the old sailors? Do you not see that all are young men?' . . .Where are the old idealists? Where are they who represented to the last generation that extravagant hope . . . who represented genius, virtue, the invisible and heavenly world? Are they dead, taken in early ripeness to the gods . . . or did the high idea die out of them?"
—Emerson, excerpts from lecture, Boston, Masonic Hall, 1842

"During his lecture, Emerson woefully acknowledged that the goal of a purely transcendental outlook on life would be impossible to attain in practice."
—Wikipedia, 2016

". . . Now they tell me!"
—Kate Peters, Throwback Wilderness Wife, 2016

❀

Fallout from a Sighting

"What a sorrowful act must that be—the covering up of wells!"
—*Thoreau*

"It's about the abandonment of your dream—and the need to focus on a new dream—no matter how much effort you poured into the old one."
—*Karen Olanna, Alaskan Artist*

"Inside every cynical person is a disappointed idealist."
—*George Carlin, Comedian*

✺

"Are You a Cynical Idealist?"

The basic concept of idealism is essentially one of transcendence: either pursuing—or desiring, wishing, or even longing for—what doesn't yet exist (if in fact, it ever can).

After pursuing high or noble principles, [comes] a disenchantment with what had earlier been believed or sought after.

So how, exactly, do so many people move from a pure, untainted idealism—which, purportedly, is intrinsic to our nature—to a far more nuanced (and negative) "cynical idealism"?

Ironically, such a conceptual degradation is a natural outgrowth of this far more utopian, though ultimately untenable (or quixotic) stance. It's moving from what might be designated a "romantic," or unconditionally idealistic stance toward a more sophisticated and realistic one.

And it results from a combination of formal and informal education, growing maturation, and an ever-evolving, level-headed assessment of experience.

. . . Adopting the viewpoint of the cynical idealist makes a great deal of sense. It's a modified, necessarily self-protective stance in the face of a world that routinely doesn't operate in accordance with any of our golden-rule principles.

—Leon F. Seltzer, *"Are You a Cynical Idealist?"*
Psychology Today, *February 28, 2018*

"The best people possess a feeling for beauty, the courage to take risks, the discipline to tell the truth, the capacity for sacrifice. Ironically, their virtues make them vulnerable; they are often wounded, sometimes destroyed."

—Ernest Hemingway

∗ ∗ ∗

At the time, my parents' decision to abandon the farm must have felt like failure. But life is what it is, and Mama assures me that their retro-style endeavor was *not* a failure. Instead, she says that their Alaskan adventure was the crowning glory of their lives. (Not counting having Brew and me, of course.)

"So, was it worth it?" I asked my mama. "I mean, would you two do it again?"

"*Absolutely,* we would (if we were forty years younger), because your life is the sum of all the things you do, not what you didn't do. When you're young, you can dare to reach out to grasp your dream. Wrap your heart around it. Even if you lose your grip along the way, at least you'll have memories of an exciting ride. I guess that's probably good enough."

"Some memories are realities, and are better than anything that can ever happen to one again." —*Cather*

"The Forget-me-not is Alaska's state flower. Could anyone who has ever lived within her woods, forget Alaska? I think not."
—*Kate Peters*

※

Choosing Joy

The fellow who lost a week's work when it landed in the ditch wisely concluded, "Shucks, 'twern't nothin' I won't get over. For I have seen the elephant! Ain't nothin' likely to ever top that."

—Anonymous Life Enthusiast

"Whenever you fall down, always try to come up with a mouthful of grass."

—John L. Weaver, Kate's grandfather, Farmer

"The most certain sign of wisdom is cheerfulness."
—Michel de Montaigne, 19th c. Scholar in Humanities, 1866

* * *

Well, that's it. Thanks for riding with me down my legacy trail.

May you one day forge your own adventure. And may you live to tell about it.

—Atwood Cutting, 2018

❀

"The animal merely makes a bed, which he warms with his body, in a sheltered place; but man, having discovered fire, boxes up some air in a spacious apartment, and warms that, instead of robbing himself, makes that his bed, in which he can move about divested of more cumbrous clothing, maintain a kind of summer in the midst of winter, and by means of windows even admit the light, and with a lamp lengthen out the day. Thus, he goes a step or two beyond instinct, and saves a little time for the fine arts."

—*Thoreau*

"The supreme virtue in all art is soul."

—*Cather*

✺

*"The more creatively you live your life,
the more you will experience your essential nature."*

—Lao Tzu, Taoist Sage, circa 400 BCE.

*"So live, that when thy summons comes to join
the innumerable caravan . . .
Thou go not, like the quarry-slave at night, Scourged
to his dungeon, but, sustained and soothed By an
unfaltering trust, approach thy grave
Like one who wraps the drapery of his couch
About him, and lies down to pleasant dreams."*

—William Cullen Bryant, "Thanatopsis," 1817

"Here are some suggestions.

❖ *Choose joy.*
❖ *Be kind, but protect yourself.*
❖ *If you should pray, pray for contentment.*
❖ *Do your best, and try not to leave
   too many craters behind."*

"This is my memoir and a legacy for all."

—Kate Peters

"I shall die of having lived."

—Cather

The Atwood Cutting Persona

CUTTING'S PIONEERING PARENTS—two young, idealistic, and very spontaneous souls—sledded newborn Atwood home on the back of a snow-machine. Her mother, Kate Peters, was surprised to find the nursery looking like a scene from Gettysburg, but in they went, regardless.

The author's greatest source of material for this work of historical fiction was the many stories her mother used to tell about the weather, the road, and the neighbors at the end of that impossible road. Luckily, Grandma Tutu saved all of the young pioneer's letters home to her Mamasan.

These were a gold mine. Kate Peters also took photographs and kept journals. Armed with this collection of historical documents, and embellishing the authentic narrative with reconfigured characters and homespun humor, Atwood Cutting now tells the story better than anyone else ever could—except maybe Kate Peters herself.

Educated in California, Hawaii, British Columbia, Alaska, and Vienna, Ms. Cutting graduated *Phi Beta Kappa* in Performing and Visual Arts and later felt compelled to round out her education with a Master of Liberal Arts degree in Humanities and Museum Education.

Strengthened with all of her advanced practice in Aesthetic Expression, Atwood plunged out into the job market—and found that hers might not have been the most practical of majors. Ah, well.

Today—as an artist/photographer, a storyteller and humorist, a singer, an armchair philosopher, and a bit of a poet—Atwood Cutting enjoys sharing her talents and her mother's hard-won insights with those of good hearts and willing ears.

Atwood Cutting is proud to be a member of Women Writing the West.

The complete Sleeping Moose Saga is available through
your local library.
Ingram Book Distributors
or
Amazon.com: atwood cutting: Books

See more photos and stories @ www.atwoodcutting.com

_____

Also by Atwood Cutting:
SCENIC PHOTOGRAPHY
Books designed for office waiting areas and home coffee tables.

www.ingramcontent.com/pod-product-compliance
Lightning Source LLC
Chambersburg PA
CBHW060307030426
42336CB00011B/968